QUICK & EASY

DAIRY COOKBOOK

QUICK & EASY
DAIRY COOKBOOK

EVERYDAY MEALS IN MINUTES

Executive Editor
Nick Rowe
Managing Editors
Emily Anderson, Ellen Dupont
Editor
Emma Callery
Designer
Sandra Horth

Photography
Steve Lee
Stylist
Lucy Pearce
Home Economist
Lorna Brash

Recipes created by
Pat Alburey
Joanna Farrow
Kathryn Hawkins
Sue McMahon
Kate Moseley
Victoria O'Neill

Calorie Analysis
Dr Wendy Doyle

Recipe Testing
Wendy Ambridge
Lucy Arnold
Penny Arnold
Diane Bowyer
Sarah Broad
Helen Cookson
Sandra Meadowcroft
Anne-Marie Neild

Production
Justin Masters
Printed in the EC

Eaglemoss Consumer Publications Ltd
Electra House, Crewe Business Park
Cheshire CW1 6WZ
Telephone: 01270 270 050
Website: www.dairydiary.co.uk

Front cover: **Hungarian Meatballs with Butterbeans (p122),
Raspberry Creams (p164) and Farmhouse Pasta (p50).**

Contents

Introduction

Welcome to The Quick & Easy Dairy Cookbook, *where you will find 130 quick and simple to prepare recipes. Whatever your taste and your needs, among these pages you will find a recipe to suit.*

Since 1968 when we published our first cookbook, *The Dairy Book of Home Cookery*, the Dairy Cookbooks have been helping cooks the length and breadth of the land produce delicious family meals. Over the years our books have become trusted friends, the place to go for recipes you can rely on to be tasty, economical, easy to follow and perfect every time.

As life gets ever busier, most people have less time to spend in the kitchen but still want to eat home-cooked meals. To meet today's needs, we've created *The Quick & Easy Dairy Cookbook*. Most of the 130 recipes you'll find in this book can be on the table in less than 30 minutes after you've walked into the kitchen. And for those times when you'd like to do the work in advance, we've created 24 casseroles and bakes, all of which require under 30 minutes of preparation, followed by slow cooking in the oven or on top of the stove. Set your timer and they'll be ready when you are!

Quick cooking is not only about recipes, it's about how you shop and how you do things in the kitchen. We've put together some of our favourite short cuts, handy hints and time-saving tips to help you be even quicker and more efficient in the kitchen (overleaf). And because our readers have so many favourite basic recipes from our earlier books, we've included some of these recipes on pages 184–7. Some, like the home-made mayonnaise on page 184, can be used to enhance the dishes in this book, while others, like the tomato sauce on page 186, make a quick dinner on their own when spooned over pasta. Conversion charts for dry weights, liquids and oven temperatures are provided for your reference on page 188.

The 130 recipes in this book are not only quick, they are delicious. They've been created by some of the country's leading cooks and tested in ordinary home kitchens. Every recipe uses readily available ingredients, is easy to put together and simplicity itself to serve. Whether you are creating a main course for your family during the week, something a bit more special for friends or a light bite for Saturday lunchtime, there's sure to be a recipe you'll love cooking and eating.

Left: an asparagus omelette (p 44) left flat and with the vegetables piled on top is an even quicker way of serving this delicious recipe.

RECIPE WISE

In each recipe, you'll find:

- Preparation and cooking times to help you plan your time.
- Number of servings.
- Calorie counts.
- Serving suggestions that tell you how to present the food or what to serve with it.
- Cook's tips that make food preparation easier.
- Variations that show you how to change the recipe to suit your taste.

Time savers

In today's fast-paced world, everything needs to be done as quickly as possible, not least cooking the evening meal. Learning a few simple principles will reduce the time you spend in the kitchen.

The first step is to be organised. Starting off with a tidy, well thought-out kitchen is a must for the quick cook. Keep your work surfaces clutter free, organise your drawers and cupboards so that you know exactly where everything is kept and have the equipment you use most regularly in a place where you can easily reach it. It's no good hiding the food processor away in a cupboard – getting it out will start to seem like more trouble than it's worth and you just won't make the most of its labour-saving capabilities.

Be sure to read the recipe before you start cooking. Take a look at the list of ingredients and make sure you have them all. Read the method to see the order of play. If you are using any items that are in the freezer, now is the time to get them out, thus preventing any last minute defrosting in the microwave.

Now get everything ready. By taking all the items you need out of the fridge, freezer and

TOP TIPS FOR TIME SAVING

- Keep your knives sharp, it makes chopping quicker. There are various devices you can use for sharpening – find the one that suits you best and keep it to hand.

- Declutter your kitchen drawers, it'll make things easier to find. You only need one can opener, one peeler and one masher. Keep the ones that work most efficiently and ditch the others.

- Organize your cupboards, keeping packets, tins and jars neatly ordered by type of ingredient or according to whatever system you prefer.

- Use plastic containers and baskets to help keep smaller items together.

- Turn on the oven when you walk into the kitchen.

- Boil water in the kettle rather than in a saucepan – you will find that it's much quicker.

- At the same time as boiling the water in the kettle, bring a small amount of water to the boil in a saucepan so that the pan is hot and the water from the kettle remains at boiling point when added to the pan.

- Use metal pans for cooking in as these conduct heat quickly.

- Buy meat, fish and vegetables that have been ready prepared. If you shop at your local butcher and fishmonger, you can ask him to dice or trim your meat or fillet, skin and bone your fish.

- Keep your pantry, refrigerator and freezer well stocked (see opposite).

- Double up a recipe so you can eat half now and freeze the rest for another day.

- Ensure you have a good supply of quick accompaniments such as pasta, rice, polenta and couscous in your cupboard.

- If you use chillies and ginger regularly, chop or grate lots at once, then freeze in small packages of all-purpose cling film ready to be taken out when you need them.

store cupboard you will immediately have everything to hand. But make sure you don't clutter your work surface with these items; pile them up to one side – close to but not on top of where you are working.

Some of the quickest dinners don't even need a recipe. Something as simple as pasta with a few teaspoonfuls of pesto sauce stirred in and a bowlful of grated Cheddar cheese alongside makes a delicious meal.

Experiment with the prepared sauces in the cooking sauce section of your local supermarket and keep your favourites on hand for when you

are short of time. Amid the myriad bottles and packets you're sure to find things you like whether it's an Italian pasta sauce, a balti or tikka masala to pour over strips of chicken, something with a Chinese flavour to serve with noodles or rice or a Mexican-style and taco seasoning mix.

And a quick dinner needn't leave you deprived of dessert. To finish your meal, keep a supply of ice cream in the freezer and serve with fresh fruit or chocolate sauce, either from a bottle or using our recipe for instant chocolate sauce (see page 187).

MICROWAVE TIME SAVERS

A microwave can help speed up the cooking process – and it can save on washing up. So, use your microwave to:

- Soften or melt butter.

- Melt chocolate.

- Defrost a frozen lemon (just 1 minute on High).

- Soften a lemon to get extra juice out of it (30 seconds on High).

- Cook frozen vegetables such as peas and sweetcorn.

- Defrost bread, meat, fish and leftovers.

THE QUICK COOK'S PANTRY

A well-stocked fridge, freezer and cupboard will help you get meals on the table in minutes, even if you haven't had time to shop. There are many standard items, which we assume that you are used to keeping on hand. But the following items will help you put together a quick supper or snack.

In the fridge
- Butter, unsalted
- Cheese: e.g. mature Cheddar, Parmesan
- Crème fraiche

In the freezer
- Bread
- Herbs: e.g. basil, parsley
- Ice cream
- Puff pastry

In the storecupboard
- Anchovies
- Capers
- Chocolate sauce
- Ciabatta bread mix
- Couscous
- Curry paste
- Eggs
- Garlic
- Herbs, fresh e.g. basil, coriander, parsley

- Instant mash
- Mustard: Dijon, dry
- Noodles, polenta and gnocchi
- Oil: vegetable, extra virgin olive
- Olives: black and green
- Pasta
- Pesto sauce
- Rice
- Stock: liquid/powdered
- Tapenade
- Tomato purée
- Tomato sauce
- Vegetables, dried: mushrooms, peppers, sun-dried tomatoes
- Vinegar: white and red wine, balsamic

Light Bites

If you are looking for a midweek lunch to enjoy on your own or a healthy and delicious snack for your family at the weekend, there are choices galore in this chapter. These dishes are versatile; when paired with warmed bread or a ready-prepared salad, they make great simple suppers. Many of these recipes are also elegant enough to serve as starters when cooking for friends.

Cherry Tomato Tarts

These pretty little pastries are perfect as a snack when you don't want anything too rich, or as a simple starter before a lightweight main course.

 preparation time
15 minutes

 cooking time
15 minutes

507 Kcal per portion
Suitable for vegetarians

SERVES 4

- **Butter,** 50g (2oz)
- **Red onion,** 1 large, peeled and chopped
- **Garlic cloves,** 2, peeled and crushed
- **Black olive tapenade,** 2 tbsp
- **Salt and freshly ground black pepper**
- **Cherry tomatoes,** 350g (12oz), halved
- **Black olives,** pitted, 25g (1oz)
- **Puff pastry,** ready-made, 350g (12oz)
- **Egg,** 1, beaten

COOK'S TIP

If you're not keen on olives, use 1 tbsp sun-dried tomato paste or pesto sauce instead of the tapenade. Alternatively, stir some fresh chopped herbs or a little grated Parmesan cheese into the tomato mixture.

PLANNING AHEAD

You can prepare these tarts earlier in the day and leave on the baking sheet ready to pop in the oven.

1 Preheat the oven to 220°C/425°F/Gas 7. Grease a large baking sheet. Melt the butter in a frying pan, add the onion and sauté for 2 minutes, stirring. Stir in the garlic, tapenade and a little seasoning and then the cherry tomatoes and olives and cook for about 5 minutes until the tomatoes have softened.

2 Roll out the pastry on a lightly floured surface. Cut out four 15cm (6in) rounds using a saucer or small bowl as a guide.

3 Transfer the rounds to the baking sheet. Using a sharp knife, cut a shallow circle, 1cm (½in) in from the edge. Pile the tomato mixture into the centre of each tart, keeping the mixture within the marked rim. Brush the rims with beaten egg to glaze.

4 Put in the oven and bake for about 15 minutes until the pastry is well risen and golden. Serve warm or cold.

Garlicky Mushrooms on Walnut Bread

So easy to assemble, this recipe is hearty enough to provide a light meal, particularly if you serve it with a leafy, dressed salad.

 preparation time
10 minutes

 cooking time
10 minutes

333 Kcal per portion
Suitable for vegetarians

SERVES 4

- **Butter,** 50g (2oz)
- **Olive oil,** 1 tbsp
- **Garlic cloves,** 4,
  peeled and thinly sliced
- **Chestnut mushrooms,**
  450g (1lb), quartered
- **Walnut bread,** 4 chunky
  slices
- **Flat leaf parsley,** roughly
  chopped, 4 tbsp
- **Lemon juice,** 1 tbsp
- **Salt and freshly ground
  black pepper**
- **Single cream or crème
  fraîche,** 6 tbsp
- **Flat leaf parsley,** extra,
  to garnish

1 Melt the butter with the oil in a large frying pan. Add the garlic cloves and mushrooms and fry for about 5 minutes, stirring frequently, until the mushrooms are softened.

2 While the mushrooms are cooking toast the bread in a toaster or under the grill lightly on both sides.

3 Add the parsley, lemon juice and seasoning to the mushrooms and stir for 1 minute. Stir in the cream or crème fraîche and cook for about 1 minute until heated through.

4 Pile the mushroom mixture over the toast on warmed serving plates. Serve scattered with extra parsley.

COOK'S TIP
When cooking with cream, never allow it to boil because the result is an unpleasantly curdled mixture.

Creamy Mushroom Pots with Butterbean Salad

The bean salad complements the creamy mushrooms and makes them more of a meal. For a lighter snack you could serve them with a green salad.

 preparation time
5 minutes

 cooking time
25 minutes

733 Kcal per portion
Suitable for vegetarians

SERVES 4

- **Butter,** 25g (1oz)
- **Chestnut mushrooms,** 225g (8oz), sliced
- **Salt and freshly ground black pepper**
- **Egg yolks,** 2
- **Double cream,** 300ml (½ pint)
- **Mild curry paste,** 1 rounded tsp
- **Paprika** (optional)
- **Naan breads,** 4
- **Butterbeans,** 215g can, drained
- **Red pepper, ready roasted or grilled,** 110g (4oz), sliced
- **Aubergine, ready roasted or grilled,** 110g (4oz), sliced
- **Tomatoes,** 2, sliced

1 Preheat the oven to 160°C/325°F/Gas 3. Use a little butter to lightly grease 4 deep ramekins.

2 Heat a frying pan, add the rest of the butter and sauté the mushrooms for 4–5 minutes. Season well and divide them between the ramekins, keeping 12 slices back for garnish. Put the ramekins on a baking tray.

3 Whisk the egg yolks, cream and curry paste and pour into the ramekins. Put in the oven and bake for about 20 minutes until the custard is just set. Garnish with the reserved mushrooms and sprinkle with black pepper or paprika, if you like.

4 Meanwhile, put the naan breads in the oven to warm for 10 minutes and put the butterbeans, red pepper, aubergine and tomato in the frying pan and warm through for 5 minutes.

5 Serve the mushroom pots on large plates with the naan breads and warm salad dressed with some of the oil from the aubergine or pepper jar.

COOK'S TIP

Ready roasted red pepper and aubergine is available in supermarkets in jars. You can usually find them with the ready-made sauces.

VARIATIONS

Korma curry paste is the mildest type, adding a very subtle flavour to the custard. If you prefer, the custards could be cooked plain or flavoured with nutmeg or paprika instead of the korma curry paste.

If you can get fresh wild mushrooms, try them in this recipe for a starter for a special meal.

For the salad dressing, use 1 tbsp olive oil mixed with 1 tsp lemon juice for something a bit lighter than the oil from the jar.

Roasted Red Peppers with Goat's Cheese

Roasting peppers really brings out their deliciously sweet flavour, creating a perfect contrast to the salty, smooth, melting cheese.

 preparation time
5 minutes

 cooking time
25 minutes

337 Kcal per portion
Suitable for vegetarians

COOK'S TIPS

If you are serving the peppers as a starter prior to a hearty main course, halve the portions.

When roasting vegetables it is best to get the oven really hot so they get lightly charred as they cook.

SERVES 4

- **Red peppers**, 4, cored, halved and deseeded
- **Red onions**, 2, peeled and finely sliced
- **Fresh thyme**, chopped, 1 tbsp
- **Olive oil**, 4 tbsp
- **Caster sugar**, 2 tsp
- **Salt and freshly ground black pepper**
- **Firm goat's cheese**, 200g (7oz)
- **Lemon juice**, 1 tbsp

1 Preheat the oven to 230°C/450°F/Gas 8. Place the peppers cut sides up in a roasting tin and pile the onions in the centres. Scatter with the thyme, olive oil and sugar and season lightly. Roast for 20 minutes.

2 Thinly slice the cheese, arrange over the onions and drizzle with the lemon juice. Return to the oven for about 5 minutes until the cheese is melting. Serve hot.

Eggs Benedict

A short-cut Hollandaise sauce makes a wonderful topping for ham and eggs.
Piled onto toasted muffins, this really is the ultimate light lunch or snack.

preparation time
5 minutes

cooking time
20 minutes

589 Kcal per portion

SERVES 4

- **Butter**, 150g (5oz), chilled
- **Egg yolks**, 2
- **Lemon juice**, 1 tbsp
- **Salt and freshly ground black pepper**
- **Eggs**, 4
- **Wholemeal or white muffins**, 4, split
- **Smoked ham**, 4 thick slices

1 To make the Hollandaise sauce, bring a small saucepan containing a 2cm (¾in) depth of water, to a simmer. Place a heatproof bowl over the pan, making sure the base of the bowl doesn't touch the water.

2 Half fill another saucepan with water and bring to the boil, ready for poaching the eggs. Cut the butter into small pieces.

3 Add the yolks to the bowl and whisk to break them up. Add a piece of butter and whisk into the yolks until melted. Add more butter, a piece at a time, whisking in until melted – about 10 minutes. Once all the butter is incorporated, add the lemon juice and a little seasoning. Turn off the heat and cover the bowl with a saucepan lid to keep the sauce warm.

4 Break the eggs into the simmering water and leave for about 2 minutes until just cooked (poached). Toast the muffins.

5 Place the muffins on warmed serving plates and top with a piece of smoked ham. Using a slotted spoon, drain and place a poached egg on the ham. Pour over the sauce and serve.

COOK'S TIPS

If the sauce thickens once made, add a few drops of boiling water to thin the consistency.

For flavour variations, stir a little mustard into the sauce before pouring over the eggs.

Red Bean & Squash Soup

This chunky soup makes a perfect warming winter starter.

preparation time
10 minutes

cooking time
20 minutes

227 Kcal per portion
Suitable for vegetarians

SERVES 4

- **Butternut squash,** 1kg (2lb 4oz)
- **Vegetable oil,** 2 tbsp
- **Fresh thyme,** 1 tbsp
- **Dried chilli flakes,** ½ tsp
- **Ground coriander,** 2 tsp
- **Red onion,** 1 large, peeled and chopped
- **Dark muscovado sugar,** 2 tsp
- **Vegetable stock,** 750ml (1¼ pints)
- **Red kidney beans,** 400g can, rinsed and drained
- **Coriander,** 15g (½oz), roughly chopped, except for a few leaves
- **Salt and freshly ground black pepper**
- **Greek-style natural yogurt,** to serve

1 Halve the squash. Scoop out the seeds and discard. Cut the squash into thick slices then trim away the skin from each slice. Roughly chop the flesh.

2 Heat the oil in a large saucepan. Add the squash, thyme, spices and onion and fry for 5 minutes, stirring until the vegetables are lightly coloured.

3 Add the sugar and stock and bring to the boil. Reduce the heat, cover with a lid and simmer gently for 10–15 minutes until the squash is tender. Stir in the red kidney beans and then cook for 2 minutes.

4 Using a hand-held electric wand, or a potato masher if you prefer, pulp the soup lightly until the squash and the beans are broken up but still chunky.

5 Stir in the fresh coriander, reserving the leaves for garnish, and season to taste. Ladle the soup into warmed bowls and serve topped with spoonfuls of yogurt and the remaining coriander.

VARIATIONS
Add half a diced red pepper and half a diced orange pepper to the yogurt for a crunchy change of pace.

COOK'S TIP
To transform the soup into a main meal soup, fry some chopped bacon with the onions and add a chopped potato with the squash.

Robust Spanish Country Soup

A few good quality ingredients cooked simply makes this a really nourishing soup – and there's enough for second helpings.

 preparation time
10 minutes

 cooking time
20 minutes

239 Kcal per portion

SERVES 4

- **Chicken stock cubes**, 2
- **Potatoes**, 2, thinly sliced
- **Onion**, 1, peeled and thinly sliced
- **Chorizo Spanish sausage**, 150g (5oz) piece, skinned
- **Savoy cabbage**, 175g (6oz), finely shredded
- **Parsley**, a good handful, roughly chopped

COOK'S TIP
Chorizo sausage is a Spanish speciality that is always handy to have in the fridge. It keeps for a few weeks and can be added to pasta, risottos and chicken dishes for an instant Mediterranean taste.

1 Pour 1.3 litres (2¼ pints) boiling water into a large saucepan, whisk in the stock cubes and then add the potato and onion slices. Cover, bring to the boil and simmer for 10 minutes.

2 Cut the chorizo into 5mm (¼in) slices and then chunks. Heat a small frying pan, add the chorizo and fry until browned and the oil has run out – about 5 minutes. With a draining spoon, add the chorizo to the soup but reserve the pink oil.

3 Put the cabbage on top of the simmering water. Push it down a little but don't stir it in, just let it steam for 3–4 minutes, uncovered, until just tender, but still bright green. Stir in the cabbage and season well.

4 Ladle the soup into warmed soup bowls, drizzle the chorizo oil over each bowl and finally sprinkle with the parsley. Serve the soup immediately.

Leek & Potato Soup

Leeks make a delicious soup either on their own or mixed with other vegetables. This classic combination makes a nourishing dish at any time of the year.

**preparation time
5 minutes**

**cooking time
25 minutes**

279 Kcal per portion
Suitable for vegetarians

SERVES 4

- **Butter,** 50g (2oz)
- **Leeks,** 4, rinsed and sliced
- **Onion,** 1, peeled and chopped
- **Potatoes,** 2 small, cut into small chunks
- **Vegetable stock,** 1 litre (1¾ pints)
- **Single cream,** 150ml (¼ pint)
- **Salt and freshly ground black pepper**
- **Nutmeg,** freshly grated
- **Chives,** handful, to garnish

1 Melt the butter in a large saucepan. Add the leeks and onion and fry gently, stirring frequently, for 5 minutes until softened.

2 Add the potatoes and stock and bring to the boil. Reduce the heat, cover with a lid and simmer gently for 15 minutes until the potatoes are very tender.

3 Using a hand-held electric wand, blend the soup until the vegetables are finely chopped but not completely smooth. Stir in 100ml (3½fl oz) of the cream and season to taste.

4 Ladle the soup into bowls and swirl with the remaining cream. Grate a little nutmeg over the soup and add some snipped chives to serve.

COOK'S TIP

If you prefer a completely smooth soup, blend it in a food processor or liquidiser, then return it to the pan and add the cream. Don't allow the soup to boil once the cream has been added otherwise it may curdle.

FREEZING

Transfer any leftovers to a freeze-proof container, chill overnight and put in the freezer the next day.

Thai Chicken Noodle Soup

This is a really quick and easy version of a spicy Thai style soup with all the aromatic fragrance of the real thing.

 preparation time
10 minutes

 cooking time
20 minutes

473 Kcal per portion

SERVES 4

- **Boneless chicken thighs,** 8 small, skinned
- **Butter,** 50g (2oz)
- **Green chilli,** 1, cored, deseeded and roughly chopped
- **Lime,** 1, finely grated zest and juice
- **Coriander,** 25g (1oz)
- **Garlic cloves,** 3, peeled and roughly chopped
- **Root ginger,** 40g (1½oz), peeled and roughly chopped
- **Spring onions,** 1 bunch, trimmed and sliced diagonally
- **Red pepper,** 1 small, cored, deseeded and finely sliced
- **Chicken stock,** 900ml (1½ pints)
- **Creamed coconut,** 75g (3oz), roughly chopped
- **Caster sugar,** 1 tbsp
- **Pak choi,** 200g (7oz), shredded
- **Stir-fry rice noodles,** 100g (3½oz)
- **Salt**
- **Lime,** 1, cut into wedges, for serving

COOK'S TIP
If you can't find pak choi use 200g (7oz) Savoy cabbage instead, shredding the leaves in the same way.

VARIATION
Fresh prawns are a nice addition to this soup – add 8 large raw prawns at the same time as the pak choi and noodles.

1 Thinly slice the chicken thighs. Melt the butter in a large saucepan and fry the chicken gently for 5 minutes, stirring frequently to prevent the chicken from sticking.

2 While the chicken is cooking put the chilli, lime zest and juice, coriander (reserving some for garnishing), garlic and ginger in a food processor and blend until finely chopped, scraping the mixture down from the sides of the bowl if necessary.

3 Add the mixture to the pan together with the spring onions, red pepper, stock, coconut and sugar. Bring the mixture gently to the boil then reduce the heat and simmer gently for 5 minutes.

4 Add the pak choi and noodles and salt, to taste. Simmer very gently for 3–5 minutes until the noodles are soft. Serve immediately garnished with the remaining coriander and with wedges of lime to squeeze over.

Minted Pea & Bacon Soup

Sweet, minty peas and salty bacon make a really appetising combination in this smooth, creamy soup.

 preparation time
5 minutes

 cooking time
20 minutes

226 Kcal per portion

SERVES 6

- **Butter,** 15g (½oz)
- **Olive oil,** 1 tbsp
- **Smoked bacon rashers,** 4, chopped into small pieces
- **Onion,** 1 large, peeled and chopped
- **Frozen peas,** 400g (14oz)
- **Vegetable stock,** 1.3 litres (2½ pints)
- **Mint sprigs,** 3, chopped
- **Single cream,** 150ml (¼ pint)
- **Freshly ground black pepper**
- **Extra mint sprigs,** to garnish
- **Spring onion,** 1, shredded, to garnish

1 Melt the butter with the oil in a large saucepan. Add the bacon and onion and fry gently for 5 minutes until both are beginning to colour.

2 Add the peas and stock and bring to the boil. Reduce the heat, cover and simmer gently for 10 minutes. Stir in the mint, then transfer to a food processor or liquidiser and blend until the liquid is smooth.

3 Return to the pan and add all of the cream. Heat through gently, adding a little pepper to taste.

4 Ladle into bowls and serve garnished with mint leaves and a handful of shredded spring onion.

COOK'S TIP
Take care when seasoning this soup, particularly if you've used stock cubes. The saltiness of the bacon and stock will probably mean that you won't need any extra salt.

Mediterranean Tomato & Pepper Soup

This makes a really pretty soup, deep red and speckled with fresh, fragrant basil.

 preparation time
8 minutes

 cooking time
15 minutes

163 Kcal per portion
Suitable for vegetarians

SERVES 4

- **Olive oil**, 3 tbsp
- **Red peppers**, 2, cored, deseeded and roughly chopped
- **Red onion**, 1 small, peeled and roughly chopped
- **Garlic clove**, 1, peeled and roughly chopped
- **Chopped tomatoes**, 400g can
- **Sun-dried tomato paste**, 2 tbsp
- **Vegetable stock**, 750ml (1¼ pints)
- **Basil**, 25g (1oz)
- **Salt and freshly ground black pepper**
- **Crème fraîche**, to serve

VARIATION
Use 4 very ripe tomatoes in place of the canned variety. Skin and roughly chop them before adding to the peppers.

1 Heat the olive oil in a large saucepan. Add the red peppers and onion and fry gently for 5 minutes. Add the garlic, tomatoes, tomato paste and stock and bring to the boil. Reduce the heat and cook gently for 2 minutes.

2 Blend the mixture in two batches in a food processor, adding some of the basil with each batch. Return to the saucepan and reheat gently, seasoning to taste.

3 To serve, ladle into bowls and top with spoonfuls of crème fraîche and a grind of black pepper.

Mussels with Crème Fraîche & Mixed Herbs

Mussels have such a wonderful flavour that it's best to cook them really simply, adding some herbs and crème fraîche to the cooking juices.

 preparation time
10 minutes

 cooking time
12 minutes

290 Kcal per portion

SERVES 4

- **Fresh mussels,** 1kg (2lb 4oz)
- **Butter,** 25g (1oz)
- **Shallots,** 3, finely chopped
- **Garlic cloves,** 3, peeled and thinly sliced
- **Dry white wine,** 150ml (¼ pint)
- **Flat leaf parsley,** 15g (½oz), chopped
- **Fennel or tarragon,** 15g (½oz), chopped
- **Crème fraîche,** 200g (7oz)
- **Salt and freshly ground black pepper**
- **Chopped herbs,** extra, to garnish

1 Scrub the mussels thoroughly under cold running water, removing any beards that cling to the shell. Discard any damaged shells or any open shells that do not close when tapped firmly with the back of a knife.

2 Melt the butter in a large saucepan. Add the shallots and fry gently for 3 minutes until softened. Add the garlic and wine and bring to the boil.

3 Tip the mussels into the pan, cover with a tight-fitting lid and cook for 3–4 minutes, shaking the pan frequently, until the mussel shells have opened wide. Using a slotted spoon, scoop out the mussels into a bowl, discarding any that have not opened. Keep warm.

4 Add the herbs, crème fraîche and a little seasoning to the pan and bring to the boil. Boil for about 2 minutes until the sauce has thickened slightly. Return the mussels and any drained juices to the pan and stir until lightly coated in the sauce.

5 Ladle onto large plates or bowls and spoon over any sauce left in the pan. Serve immediately, sprinkled with extra herbs.

COOK'S TIP
The juices from these mussels are so delicious that it is good to serve this dish with plenty of crusty bread for mopping them up.

VARIATION
This quantity will serve four people as a starter and two as a main course. If serving four as a main course, double all the quantities.

Beetroot, New Potato & Smoked Fish Salad

Colourful, crisp and refreshing, this healthy salad is packed with vibrant flavours for a lovely summery snack or starter.

 preparation time
10 minutes

 cooking time
20 minutes

572 Kcal per portion

SERVES 4

- **Olive oil,** 6 tbsp
- **Red wine vinegar,** 3 tbsp
- **Caster sugar,** 2 tsp
- **Grainy mustard,** 2 tsp
- **Salt and freshly ground black pepper**
- **New potatoes,** 450g (1lb)
- **Eggs,** 4
- **Sugarsnap peas,** 100g (3½oz)
- **Spring onions,** ½ bunch, trimmed and thinly sliced
- **Smoked mackerel,** 250g (9oz)
- **Beetroot,** raw, 1 small

1 To make the dressing, mix together the oil, vinegar, sugar and mustard in a small bowl or jar. Season to taste and set aside.

2 Scrub the potatoes and halve if large. Put in a saucepan, cover with cold water and add a little salt. Bring to the boil, reduce the heat and then leave to simmer gently for 15 minutes until tender. Cook the eggs in a small saucepan of gently simmering water for 8 minutes.

3 Meanwhile, shred the sugarsnap peas and put in a salad bowl with the spring onions. Discard the skin from the fish and roughly flake into the bowl.

4 Peel the beetroot and slice very thinly. Then thinly slice in the opposite direction to make matchstick-sized pieces.

5 Drain the potatoes well. Drain and peel the eggs and slice roughly. Add to the bowl with the dressing and fold the ingredients gently together. Serve on individual plates topped with the beetroot matchsticks.

COOK'S TIP
When buying the smoked mackerel choose the pepper-free variety unless you want to add a little heat to the dish.

Prawn, Mango & Crispy Bacon Salad

Tangy mangoes, sweet prawns and salty bacon combine in a modern take on the classic prawn cocktail.

 preparation time
10 minutes

 cooking time
8 minutes

272 Kcal per portion

SERVES 4

- **Low-fat natural fromage frais**, 2 tbsp
- **Mayonnaise**, 2 tbsp
- **Mild curry powder**, ½ tsp
- **Large ripe mango**, 1
- **Large peeled prawns**, cooked, 350g (12oz)
- **Butter**, 15g (½oz)
- **Unsmoked, rindless streaky bacon rashers**, 4
- **Watercress**, 1 bunch, washed and dried
- **Freshly ground black pepper**
- **Lime**, 1, cut into wedges

VARIATIONS

These quantities make enough for a light meal. Reduce the quantities for a starter.

For a lower-calorie version, use back bacon, omit the butter and grill the rashers until crisp.

1 Mix together the fromage frais, mayonnaise and curry powder in a small bowl. Cover and chill until required.

2 Peel the mango and slice down either side of the smooth, flat central stone. Discard the stone and chop the flesh roughly and place in a bowl. Wash and pat dry the prawns and mix into the mango. Set aside.

3 Melt the butter in a frying pan and fry the bacon for 3–4 minutes on each side until it is golden and crispy. Remove from the pan, drain well and then chop finely. Toss into the mango and prawns along with the watercress.

4 To serve, pile the salad onto serving plates. Top each serving with a dollop of curried mayonnaise and season with black pepper. Serve with wedges of lime to squeeze over.

Tuna Steaks with Bean Salad

*This makes a simple but stylish
light lunch dish for friends.*

 preparation time
10 minutes

 cooking time
8 minutes

423 Kcal per portion

SERVES 4

- **Fresh tuna steaks**, 4, weighing 150g (5oz) each
- **Salt and freshly ground black pepper**
- **Cannellini beans**, 300g can
- **Cherry tomatoes**, 150g (5oz), quartered
- **Spring onions**, 2, trimmed and finely sliced
- **Cumin seeds**, 1 tsp, lightly crushed
- **Caster sugar**, 2 tsp
- **Lemon juice**, 2 tbsp
- **Coriander**, 25g (1oz), roughly chopped
- **Extra virgin olive oil**, 4 tbsp
- **Butter**, 25g (1oz)

COOK'S TIP

For a hearty main course use 200g (7oz) tuna steaks and serve
with plenty of warm, grainy bread and a green salad.

PLANNING AHEAD

The salad can be made several hours in advance and chilled so all
the flavours mingle together. But remove from the refrigerator an
hour before serving as the salad should not be served ice cold.

1 Pat the tuna steaks dry on kitchen paper and season on both sides.

2 Rinse and drain the cannellini beans and put in a large bowl with the tomatoes, spring onions, cumin, sugar, lemon juice, coriander and 3 tbsp of the oil. Add a little seasoning and toss the ingredients together.

3 Melt the butter with the remaining oil in a frying pan. Add the tuna steaks and fry quickly for 1–2 minutes on each side until they turn golden.

4 Pile the bean salad onto serving plates and top with the tuna steaks, drizzling over any buttery juices left in the pan.

Warm Mexican Chicken Salad

This is a colourful main meal salad that offers a wealth of flavours and textures.

 preparation time
10 minutes

 cooking time
10 minutes

670 Kcal per portion

SERVES 4

- **Boneless chicken breasts,** 450g (1lb), skinned
- **Hot chilli powder,** ½ tsp
- **Paprika,** 1 tbsp
- **Dried onion powder,** 1 tsp
- **Salt and freshly ground black pepper**
- **Vegetable oil,** 2 tbsp
- **Red onion,** 1, peeled and finely chopped
- **Sweetcorn kernels,** 326g can, drained and rinsed
- **Kidney beans,** 420g can, drained and rinsed
- **Coriander,** a few sprigs
- **Prepared assorted baby salad leaves,** 110g (4oz)
- **Avocados,** 2
- **Lime,** 1, juice
- **Tortilla chips,** 110g (4oz)
- **Soured cream,** 150ml (¼ pint), to serve

VARIATION

For a low-calorie version, replace the soured cream with low-fat natural fromage frais and omit the tortilla chips.

1 Wash and pat dry the chicken, then cut into narrow strips. Place the chicken in a bowl and toss in the chilli powder, paprika, onion powder and seasoning.

2 Heat the oil in a large frying pan or wok and stir-fry the chicken for 7–8 minutes until the chicken is thoroughly cooked and golden. Drain well and keep warm.

3 Place the onion in a serving bowl with the sweetcorn, kidney beans, coriander (reserving some of the leaves for garnishing) and finally the salad leaves. Halve the avocados, remove the stone and peel away the skin. Cut the flesh into thick wedges and toss in the juice from the lime.

4 To serve, toss the avocado and warm chicken into the salad, along with the tortilla chips, and serve immediately with soured cream to spoon over.

Herby Chicken Couscous

A large bunch of fresh herbs make this a wonderfully summery salad.

 preparation time
10 minutes

 cooking time
12 minutes

578 Kcal per portion

SERVES 4

- **Couscous**, 225g (8oz)
- **Hot chicken or vegetable stock**, 300ml (½ pint)
- **Boneless chicken breasts**, 4 small, skinned
- **Salt and freshly ground black pepper**
- **Pine nuts**, 50g (2oz)
- **Butter**, 25g (1oz)
- **Olive oil**, 5 tbsp
- **Mint**, 15g (½oz), chopped
- **Flat-leaf parsley**, 15g (½oz), chopped
- **Celery**, 2 sticks, chopped
- **Garlic cloves**, 3, peeled and thinly sliced
- **Sultanas**, 75g (3oz)
- **Lemon juice**, 2 tbsp

VARIATION

For a main course salad, use large chicken breasts and double the quantity of the rest of the ingredients.

1 Put the couscous in a large bowl, add the hot stock and leave for 5 minutes. Slice each chicken breast lengthways with diagonal cuts into 5 thin slices and season.

2 Heat a large frying pan, add the pine nuts and heat for about 2 minutes until toasted. Tip them over the couscous.

3 Add the butter and 1 tbsp of the oil to the frying pan and heat until the butter has melted. Add half the chicken pieces and cook for 3–4 minutes on each side until cooked through. Drain and cook the remainder.

4 Meanwhile, add the mint, parsley, celery, garlic and sultanas to the couscous and season. Toss the ingredients together. Mix the remaining olive oil in a small bowl with the lemon juice. Spoon the couscous onto serving plates, pile the chicken slices on top and drizzle with the lemon dressing to serve.

Fruity Coronation Chicken

Traditionally served in a rich, spicy mayonnaise, this version of one of our classic salads is lighter on the calories, but still packed with flavour.

**preparation time
10 minutes**

303 Kcal per portion

SERVES 4

- **Cooked chicken**, 450g (1lb), skinned
- **Ripe peaches**, 4
- **Low-fat natural fromage frais**, 4 tbsp
- **Low-calorie mayonnaise**, 2 tbsp
- **Mild curry paste**, 2 tsp
- **Spicy mango chutney**, 1 tbsp
- **Salt and freshly ground black pepper**
- **Coriander**, a few sprigs
- **Prepared assorted salad leaves**, 110g (4oz)
- **Toasted flaked almonds**, 15g (½oz)
- **Poppadums**, 2

1 Cut the chicken into bite-sized pieces and place in a bowl. Wash and pat dry the peaches, then halve them and remove the stones. Slice into thin wedges.

2 Mix together the fromage frais, mayonnaise, curry paste, chutney and seasoning. Carefully stir into the cooked chicken along with the peaches until well mixed.

3 Mix the coriander and salad leaves and put onto a serving dish. Top with the chicken and sprinkle with the flaked almonds. Lightly crush the poppadums and pile on top to serve.

PLANNING AHEAD

You can make this salad in advance. Simply prepare the curried chicken and peach mixture (but leave the poppadums until serving or they will get soggy), and cover and chill it until required. Then continue with the recipe when you are ready to serve the salad.

Chicken Liver & Rosemary Pâté

*Chopped fresh rosemary and tangy pickled walnuts give
a classic chicken liver pâté added interest.*

 preparation time
5 minutes

 cooking time
25 minutes

354 Kcal per portion

SERVES 6

- **Butter**, 75g (3oz)
- **Onion**, 1 large, peeled
  and chopped
- **Chicken livers**, 2 x 225g
  tubs, rinsed and drained
- **Garlic cloves**, 2, peeled
  and roughly chopped
- **Rosemary**, 6 long sprigs,
  chopped
- **Marsala or sherry**, 6 tbsp
- **Salt and freshly ground
  black pepper**
- **Pickled walnuts**, 150g
  (5oz), drained
- **Rosemary sprigs**,
  to garnish

PLANNING AHEAD

This is a really straightforward
snack or simple starter to make
ahead of time.

FREEZING

If you are cooking this recipe
ahead of time, freeze the
mixture in little pots, thawing
overnight in the fridge.

1 Melt the butter in a large frying pan. Add the onion and
chicken livers and fry gently for about 10 minutes, stirring
frequently until cooked through.

2 Add the garlic, rosemary, Marsala or sherry and seasoning
and leave to cool for 5 minutes. Tip the mixture into a food
processor and blend until smooth and creamy, scraping the
mixture down from the sides of the bowl if necessary. (You'll
probably need to blend the mixture in two batches.) Put the
blended pâté in a mixing bowl.

3 Chop the pickled walnuts into small pieces and add to the
mixture. Stir until evenly combined. Turn the pâté into a
serving dish or individual ramekins and chill until ready to serve.

4 Serve garnished with rosemary sprigs and, for a starter, serve
with a few salad leaves and pretty curls of melba toast or, for
a more substantial dish, with chunkier toast.

Weekday Dinners

When time is precious and the day has been a busy
one, the last thing you want is to spend hours
in the kitchen. With your hectic lifestyle in mind, we
offer a selection of dishes that you can have on the
table in less than 30 minutes. Whatever your
taste – vegetarian fare, a warming bowl of pasta, light
and healthy fish, or a meat dish to get your teeth into –
you will find plenty of choice for all the family here.

Creamy Mushroom Crepes

Not just for Shrove Tuesday, these cheese-topped, mushroom-stuffed pancakes make a delicious weekday supper dish anytime.

 preparation time
15 minutes

 cooking time
15 minutes

714 Kcal per portion
Suitable for vegetarians

SERVES 4

- **Butter,** 75g (3oz)
- **Button mushrooms,** 350g (12oz), wiped and sliced
- **Flour,** 1 tbsp
- **Milk,** 450ml (¾ pint)
- **Mustard powder,** ½ tsp
- **Parsley,** chopped, 2 tbsp
- **Salt and freshly ground black pepper**
- **Mature Cheddar cheese,** 175g (6oz), grated
- **Pancakes,** 8 ready-made, defrosted if frozen

1 Melt 50g (2oz) of the butter in a deep frying pan. Add the mushrooms and cook for 4–5 minutes, stirring occasionally, until the mushrooms have softened and are starting to brown. Remove from the pan.

2 Melt the remaining butter in the pan and add the flour. Blend together and cook for 1–2 minutes, then gradually add the milk, beating well and allowing the mixture to come to the boil between each addition.

3 Simmer the sauce gently for a couple of minutes, then stir in the cooked mushrooms, mustard, parsley and seasoning. Stir in half of the Cheddar cheese.

4 Preheat the grill to hot and butter a Swiss-roll tin. Divide the mushroom mix between the pancakes, and roll up each one.

5 Place the rolled-up pancakes on the Swiss-roll tin with the seams underneath and so that they are touching each other.

6 Sprinkle over the remaining Cheddar cheese and then place under the grill until the cheese melts and turns golden. Serve immediately with a green salad.

VARIATION

For a more substantial meal, add some chopped, cooked chicken, bacon or ham to the sauce. For a starter, serve just one pancake per person.

Leek & Wensleydale Tartlets

Crisp, flaky pastry, smooth, silky leeks and rich, tangy cheese make a delicious combination.

preparation time
15 minutes

cooking time
10 minutes

457 Kcal per portion
Suitable for vegetarians

SERVES 4

- **Ready-rolled puff pastry,** 375g (13oz)
- **Leek,** 1, large, washed and sliced
- **Oil,** 2 tbsp
- **Salt and freshly ground black pepper**
- **Wensleydale cheese,** 2 thick slices

COOK'S TIP
Keep ready-cut puff pastry circles in the freezer and take them out when needed – don't bother to defrost. Place on a greased tray, add a topping and place straight into a hot oven. Try thinly sliced raw red onion and tomatoes topped with a sprinkling of fresh herbs and a drizzle of olive oil – couldn't be quicker.

1 Preheat the oven to 230°C/450°F/Gas 8 and oil a baking sheet. Roll out the puff pastry to make it a little bigger and cut out 4 x 13cm (5in) diameter circles. Lay the pastry circles on the baking sheet and prick the centres with a fork.

2 Put the sliced leek in a saucepan with 1 tbsp of oil and sufficient water to cover the leeks. Cover the pan and sweat gently for 5 minutes until tender, then drain and add seasoning.

3 Pile the leeks on the pastry leaving the border free. Scatter crumbled cheese over the top, pressing everything down gently. Brush the filling and pastry edges with a little oil.

4 Bake in the oven for 10 minutes until golden. Serve immediately accompanied by green beans or a tomato salad dressed with olive oil.

Polenta-topped Ratatouille

Soft, smooth polenta takes the place of pastry as a healthy topping for this fresh-tasting ratatouille.

 preparation time
10 minutes

 cooking time
20 minutes

289 Kcal per portion
Suitable for vegetarians

SERVES 4

- **Butter,** 50g (2oz), melted
- **Olive oil,** 1 tbsp
- **Onion,** 1, peeled and sliced
- **Aubergine,** 1 small, cubed
- **Courgettes,** 2, sliced
- **Red pepper,** 1, cored, deseeded and sliced
- **Garlic clove,** 1, peeled and crushed
- **Cherry tomatoes,** 400g can
- **Basil,** chopped, 2 tbsp
- **Salt and freshly ground black pepper**
- **Polenta,** ready-made, 500g block
- **Parmesan cheese,** grated, 3 level tbsp

1 Heat half the butter and all the oil in a deep frying pan. Add the onion and cook for 4–5 minutes until the onion softens.

2 Add the aubergine, courgettes, red pepper and garlic and continue to cook for about 5 minutes, until all the vegetable have softened.

3 Add the cherry tomatoes and simmer for a further 2–3 minutes, stirring occasionally, but taking care not to break down the tomatoes too much. Stir in the basil and season to taste. Pour into a flameproof dish.

4 Preheat the grill to hot. Cut the polenta into thin slices and place over the vegetable mixture. Brush over with the remaining butter and sprinkle over the Parmesan cheese.

5 Place the dish under the grill until the cheese melts and turns a golden colour. Serve immediately.

COOK'S TIP

You can find ready-made polenta, an Italian cornmeal-based product, in most supermarkets – usually next to the dried pastas.

VARIATION

Instead of polenta, use a 400g packet of Gnocchi di patate – small potato dumplings – also usually found next to the dried pasta. Just separate into pieces and spread out on top of the ratatouille and sprinkle with the Parmesan, they don't need pre-cooking.

Spinach & Mushroom Roulade

Whether you serve this roulade hot for a family supper or cold at a picnic or buffet, you'll find it is both easy to make and delicious to eat.

preparation time
15 minutes

cooking time
15 minutes

327 Kcal per portion
Suitable for vegetarians

SERVES 4

- **Spinach leaves**, 225g (8oz)
- **Butter**, 25g (1oz)
- **Plain flour**, 25g (1oz)
- **Milk**, 300ml (½ pint)
- **Eggs**, 4, separated
- **Nutmeg**, freshly grated
- **Salt and freshly ground black pepper**

FOR THE FILLING

- **Butter**, 50g (2oz)
- **Chestnut mushrooms**, 225g (8oz), wiped and sliced
- **Garlic clove**, 1, peeled and crushed
- **Double cream**, 2 tbsp
- **Tarragon**, chopped, ½ level tbsp

1 Preheat the oven to 200°C/400°F/Gas 6. Line a Swiss-roll tin measuring 33 x 23cm (13 x 9in) with baking parchment.

2 Pour 2 tbsp water into a saucepan and bring to the boil. Add the spinach. Cover the pan and cook for 2–3 minutes, until the spinach leaves have wilted, stirring occasionally.

3 Remove the pan from the heat and strain the spinach, squeezing out any excess liquid. Roughly chop the leaves.

4 Melt the butter in a saucepan and add the flour. Beat until a smooth, thick paste forms, then gradually add the milk, beating well between each addition of liquid.

5 Simmer for 2–3 minutes, then remove the pan from the heat and leave the sauce to cool for a few minutes. Beat in the cooked spinach, egg yolks, nutmeg and seasoning.

6 Whisk the egg whites until they are stiff, then fold them gently into the spinach mixture. Pour the mixture into the lined Swiss-roll tin and spread out to the corners.

7 Bake in the middle of the oven for 12–15 minutes until just set to the touch in the centre. Remove from the oven.

8 Meanwhile, make the filling. Melt the butter in a frying pan and add the mushrooms and garlic. Cook for 4–5 minutes until the mushrooms have softened. Then stir in the double cream and tarragon and add seasoning. Warm through but don't boil the filling or the cream will curdle.

9 Tip the roulade onto a clean sheet of baking parchment. Trim the edges and spread the mushrooms over the top. Using the baking parchment to help, roll up the roulade along the short edge. Serve hot or cold.

Asparagus Omelette

Long a favourite with any cook in a hurry, an omelette becomes a truly substantial meal when vegetables and cheese are added.

 preparation time
10 minutes

 cooking time
20 minutes

383 Kcal per portion
Suitable for vegetarians

SERVES 4

- **Asparagus tips**, 200g (7oz)
- **Eggs,** 8 large
- **Salt and freshly ground black pepper**
- **Butter,** 50g (2oz)
- **Somerset goat's cheese,** 200g (7oz), roughly diced
- **Cherry tomatoes,** 8, halved or quartered

1 Blanch the asparagus tips in a saucepan of lightly salted boiling water for 3 minutes. Drain well and keep warm.

2 For each omelette, beat 2 eggs with 1 tbsp of water and some seasoning. Heat a quarter of the butter in a non-stick frying pan and when it starts to foam pour in the beaten eggs.

3 Spread the mixture round the pan and, when almost set, pile a quarter of the diced goat's cheese, asparagus pieces and tomatoes in the middle.

4 As the cheese starts to melt, fold in the edges of the omelette towards the centre (to make an open-topped square shape). When set, slide the omelette onto a hot plate and keep warm.

5 Make 3 more omelettes with the rest of the ingredients. Serve with watercress sprinkled with balsamic vinegar.

VARIATIONS

Goat's cheese melts well in this recipe, as does Somerset Brie, which is really rich and creamy. Even a hard cheese will be fine to use here, but you will need to grate it.

Spanish Omelette

The egg equivalent of a deep-pan pizza, a Spanish omelette is a good way to use up cooked potato and any other leftover vegetables you may have.

 preparation time
10 minutes

 cooking time
20 minutes

382 Kcal per portion
Suitable for vegetarians

SERVES 4

- **Butter**, 25g (1oz)
- **Olive oil**, 1 tbsp
- **Spanish onion**, 1, peeled and finely chopped
- **Garlic cloves**, 2, peeled and finely chopped
- **Green pepper**, 1, cored, deseeded and finely chopped
- **Red pepper**, 1, cored, deseeded and finely chopped
- **Cooked potato**, 450g (1lb), peeled and thinly sliced
- **Eggs**, 6, beaten
- **Salt and freshly ground black pepper**
- **Mature Cheddar cheese**, 50g (2oz), grated
- **Flat leaf parsley leaves**, handful, to garnish

COOK'S TIP
In Spain, this omelette is often served cold, cut into squares and served as a snack – perfect for a packed lunch or picnic.

1 Melt the butter with the oil in a deep frying pan and cook the onion, garlic and peppers for 5 minutes, until softened but not browned.

2 Add the potato, raise the heat, and stir-fry for a further minute until well mixed. Level off the top to evenly fill the pan.

3 Beat together the eggs and season well. Pour the eggs into the pan and reduce the heat to a gentle simmer. Cook, stirring the scrambling eggs back into the pan, then packing the mixture down, for about 10 minutes until set.

4 Slide the omelette onto a plate and then flip back into the pan with the cooked side up. Sprinkle the surface with the cheese and cook for a further 5 minutes.

5 To serve, slice into wedges and sprinkle with the parsley. Serve with crisp salad vegetables and crusty bread.

Tomato & Mushroom Toasts

A quick-and-easy savoury custard baked with cherry tomatoes and cheese is topped with a mushroom to make an elegant vegetarian main course. The Cheddar adds flavour, while the Parmesan gives an extra cheesy boost.

 preparation time
10 minutes

 cooking time
20 minutes

401 Kcal per portion
Suitable for vegetarians

SERVES 4

- **Cherry tomatoes,** 500g (1lb 2oz)
- **Spring onions,** 4, trimmed and finely chopped
- **Eggs,** 2 large
- **Plain flour,** 2 tbsp
- **Single cream,** 142ml pot
- **Salt and freshly ground black pepper**
- **Mature Cheddar cheese,** 50g (2oz), finely grated
- **Butter,** 25g (1oz), melted
- **Flat mushrooms,** 4 large, wiped
- **Bread,** 4 chunky slices
- **Parmesan cheese,** 2 tbsp, grated

1 Preheat the oven to 190°C/375°F/Gas 5. Butter a shallow ovenproof dish and put the tomatoes and spring onions in it.

2 Whisk the eggs and then whisk in the flour, cream and seasoning. Stir in the Cheddar. Pour the mixture over the onions and tomatoes in the dish and bake in the oven for about 20 minutes until just set.

3 Brush the butter all over the mushrooms and place them stalk side down in a small roasting tin. Bake for 15 minutes, turning them over halfway through cooking. Toast the bread.

4 To serve, place a slice of toast on each of 4 plates. Cut the savoury custard into 4 wedges and place a wedge on each piece of toast and then add a mushroom. Scatter the Parmesan cheese on top. A crisp, green salad would go well with this.

VARIATION

If you don't have cream or are looking for a lower-fat version, use milk in the batter instead of the cream. It will just take a little longer to set and not be quite as rich.

Green Pasta

Silky tagliatelle and a deliciously creamy sauce make the perfect counterpoint to a medley of fresh, green vegetables.

 preparation time
5 minutes

 cooking time
20 minutes

554 Kcal per portion
Suitable for vegetarians

SERVES 4

- **Fine green beans**, 110g (4oz)
- **Salt and freshly ground black pepper**
- **Leek**, 1 large
- **Fresh green tagliatelle**, 225g (8oz)
- **Fresh white tagliatelle**, 225g (8oz)
- **Butter**, 25g (1oz)
- **Courgette**, 1 large, diced
- **Artichoke hearts**, 400g can, drained and halved
- **Medium fat soft cheese with garlic and herbs**, 175g (6oz)
- **Single cream**, 4 tbsp
- **Toasted pine nuts** 25g (1oz)
- **Parsley**, chopped, 2 tbsp

1 Cut the beans into short lengths. Bring a saucepan of lightly salted water to the boil and cook the beans for 5 minutes until just tender. Drain well and set aside.

2 Meanwhile, trim the leek and split open lengthways. Rinse under cold running water to remove any trapped earth. Shake well to remove excess water, then slice finely and set aside.

3 Bring a saucepan of lightly salted water to the boil and cook the tagliatelle according to the manufacturer's instructions. Drain well and return to the pan.

4 Meanwhile, melt the butter and gently fry the leek and courgette for 4–5 minutes until just softened. Add the beans and artichoke hearts and heat through for a further minute.

5 To serve, add the soft cheese and cream to the pasta and gently stir in until it melts in the heat of the pasta. Toss in the cooked vegetables, adjust seasoning, and pile into warmed serving bowls. Sprinkle each portion with some pine nuts and chopped parsley.

Chicken Pasta with Stilton

Creamy blue Stilton cheese transforms a simple pasta dish into a fabulous feast that is guaranteed to impress.

 preparation time
5 minutes

 cooking time
20 minutes

697 Kcal per portion

SERVES 4

- **Salt and freshly ground black pepper**
- **Pasta shapes,** 300g (11oz)
- **Broccoli,** 300g (11oz)
- **Onion,** 1
- **Boneless chicken breasts,** 450g (1lb), skinned
- **Olive oil,** 2 tbsp
- **Cherry tomatoes,** 175g (6oz)
- **Stilton cheese,** 150g (5oz)
- **Double cream,** 4 tbsp

PLANNING AHEAD

To serve as a pasta bake, make the recipe as above and allow to cool. Add 4–6 tbsp milk to loosen the mixture and pile into an ovenproof baking dish. Cover and chill for up to 2 days. When ready to serve, cover with foil and bake at 190°C/375°F/Gas 5 for 25–30 minutes, until hot. Sprinkle crumbled blue cheese on top and remove the foil for the last 5 minutes to brown.

1 Bring a saucepan of salted water to the boil, add the pasta and cook according to the manufacturer's instructions.

2 Break the broccoli into small florets and, for the last 5 minutes of the pasta cooking time, place the broccoli in a steamer or large sieve over the pasta; cover and finish cooking. Drain the pasta well and return to the cooking pan. Toss in the broccoli and then set aside.

3 Meanwhile, peel and chop the onion. Slice the chicken into thin strips. Heat the oil in a large frying pan and fry the onion and chicken strips for 7–8 minutes, stirring, until golden and cooked through.

4 Halve the cherry tomatoes and add to the pan. Cook gently for 1 minute. Crumble in the Stilton cheese and add the cream. Heat through, stirring, for 1 minute until melted.

5 Finally, add the chicken and blue cheese mixture to the pasta and broccoli and stir well to mix. Heat through gently for 1–2 minutes until hot. Adjust seasoning and serve.

Farmhouse Pasta

This hearty, chunky sausage and pasta supper is bound to be popular with all the family.

 preparation time
5 minutes

 cooking time
25 minutes

731 Kcal per portion

SERVES 4

- **Thick pork sausages**, 450g (1lb)
- **Red onions**, 2 large
- **Red wine vinegar**, 2 tbsp
- **Butter**, 15g (½oz)
- **Olive oil**, 1 tbsp
- **Clear honey**, 1 tbsp
- **Pasta shapes**, 350g (12oz)
- **Salt and freshly ground black pepper**
- **Double cream**, 6 tbsp
- **Wholegrain mustard**, 2 tbsp
- **Chives**, chopped, 2 tbsp

1 Bring a large saucepan of lightly salted water to the boil. Grill the sausages according to the manufacturer's instructions.

2 Meanwhile, peel and slice the onions and toss in the vinegar. Leave to stand for 5 minutes. Melt the butter with the oil and fry the onions with the vinegar for 5 minutes until just softened.

3 Add the honey and continue to cook, stirring, for a further 5 minutes until golden. Cook the pasta in the boiling water according to the manufacturer's instructions. Drain well and return to the saucepan.

4 Cut the cooked sausages into chunks and mix into the drained pasta along with the onions and seasoning. Over a low heat stir in the cream and mustard. Heat through, stirring, for 2–3 minutes until very hot. To serve, pile into warmed serving bowls and sprinkle with chopped chives and extra black pepper if liked and serve with crusty bread and crisp salad.

Tomato & Basil Spaghetti

*Low fat needn't mean low flavour. This pasta dish is so delicious
that no one would know it's low fat unless you told them!*

 preparation time
5 minutes

 cooking time
25 minutes

372 Kcal per portion
Suitable for vegetarians

SERVES 4

- **Spaghetti**, 350g (12oz)
- **Cherry tomatoes**, 500g (1lb 2oz)
- **Olive oil**, 1 tbsp
- **Spring onions**, 8, trimmed and sliced
- **Garlic clove**, 1, peeled and crushed
- **Basil**, chopped, 2–3 tbsp
- **Salt and freshly ground black pepper**
- **Virtually fat-free fromage frais**, 150g (5oz)

COOK'S TIP
Take care not to return the saucepan to the heat after adding the fromage frais or it may curdle.

1 Bring a large saucepan of salted water to the boil and add the spaghetti. Let it soften in the steam and sink into the pan. Cook according to the manufacturer's instructions.

2 Finely chop half of the cherry tomatoes and keep to one side. Halve the remaining ones.

3 Heat the oil in a frying pan and add the halved cherry tomatoes, spring onion and garlic. Cook over a medium heat for 2–3 minutes until the tomatoes have softened slightly, then add the finely chopped tomatoes and cook for a further 1–2 minutes. Stir in the basil and plenty of seasoning.

4 Drain the pasta, return to the saucepan and stir in the tomato mixture. Remove the pan from the heat and stir in the fromage frais. Serve immediately, accompanied by crusty bread.

Pasta with Greens & Prawns

The fresh colours and flavours of spring vegetables and prawns make this a deliciously light pasta dish.

**preparation time
5 minutes**

**cooking time
20 minutes**

377 Kcal per portion

SERVES 4

- **Farfalle pasta,** 225g (8oz)
- **Sugarsnap peas,** 200g (7oz), tailed
- **Olive oil,** 1 tsp
- **Butter,** 50g (2oz)
- **Celery,** 2 sticks, finely sliced
- **Fine asparagus,** 110g (4oz), tips left whole, stalks chopped
- **Spring onions,** 6, trimmed and sliced
- **Salt and freshly ground black pepper**
- **Raw tiger prawns,** peeled, 20, defrosted if frozen
- **Garlic clove,** 1, peeled and finely chopped
- **Dill,** 2 large sprigs, to garnish

COOK'S TIP
Ready-cooked peeled prawns could be used but they're not as plump and flavoursome as raw, shell-on prawn tails or frozen, raw, peeled prawns.

1 Cook the pasta in a large saucepan of boiling salted water according to the manufacturer's instructions. For the last 4 minutes of the pasta cooking time, add the sugarsnap peas, cover and finish cooking.

2 Meanwhile, heat a frying pan, add the oil and about a third of the butter. Add the celery and chopped asparagus stalks. Stir-fry for a couple of minutes.

3 Add the spring onions and asparagus tips and stir-fry for another 2 minutes. Then add 3 tbsp of the pasta water and simmer for another few minutes. Set aside.

4 Drain the pasta and sugarsnap peas, return to the large saucepan and thoroughly stir in the pan-fried vegetables. Season and keep warm.

5 Heat the rest of the butter in the frying pan. When foaming, add the prawns in one layer and sprinkle the garlic over.

6 Turn the prawns after a couple of minutes, when they are pink underneath, and cook for 2 minutes more. Season.

7 Spoon the pasta mixture into 4 warmed bowls and divide the prawns and buttery juices between them. Tear the dill sprigs over the top to garnish.

Rice 'n' Peas with Cheese

Basic ingredients from the cupboard, fridge and freezer team up to make a delightfully creamy one-dish meal.

**preparation time
5 minutes**

**cooking time
25 minutes**

502 Kcal per portion

SERVES 4

- **Smoked streaky bacon rashers**, 8, de-rinded
- **Butter**, 25g (1oz)
- **Risotto rice**, 225g (8oz)
- **Spring onions**, 8, trimmed and chopped
- **Hot vegetable stock**, 900ml (1½ pints)
- **Frozen peas**, 200g (7oz)
- **Salt and freshly ground black pepper**
- **Mature Cheddar cheese**, 110g (4oz), roughly diced
- **Parsley**, chopped, 4 tbsp

1 Heat a large frying pan, add the bacon rashers and brown all over until they are quite crispy. Take out of the pan with tongs and set aside, keeping them warm.

2 Add the butter to the pan and when it melts, add the rice and coat it well in the butter. Stir in the spring onions and about 150ml (¼ pint) of the stock and simmer until almost all the stock has been absorbed.

3 Keeping the stock warm, gradually pour in more of it, simmering for about 20 minutes and stirring frequently until the rice is almost cooked. The mixture should not be dry.

4 Add the peas and plenty of seasoning and heat through, then add the cheese chunks. When the cheese starts to melt, sprinkle with parsley and serve with the bacon rashers cut in half and piled on top.

COOK'S TIP

The secret of a good risotto often lies in the flavour of the stock so try different brands of cubes or bottled bouillon.

VARIATIONS

For a richer, creamier dish, add a little more butter and a good sprinkling of Parmesan cheese. For a vegetarian dish, omit the bacon.

Red & Green Risotto

This risotto is full of fresh colours and flavours and makes a substantial meal. It looks great made in a shallow pan and brought straight to the table.

 preparation time
5 minutes

 cooking time
25 minutes

402 Kcal per portion
Suitable for vegetarians

SERVES 4

- **Butter,** 50g (2oz)
- **Cup mushrooms,** 110g (4oz), wiped and sliced
- **Red onion,** 1, peeled and sliced
- **Garlic cloves,** 2, peeled and finely chopped
- **Risotto rice,** 275g (10oz)
- **Sherry,** 5 tbsp
- **Hot vegetable stock,** 900ml (1½ pints)
- **Runner beans,** 110g (4oz), finely sliced
- **Ready roasted or grilled red peppers,** 110g (4oz), sliced
- **Baby spinach,** 225g bag
- **Salt and freshly ground black pepper**
- **Basil leaves,** a handful, to garnish

1 Heat a large, shallow pan, add a quarter of the butter and then the sliced mushrooms and cook for a few minutes until browned all over. Remove from the pan and keep warm.

2 Add another quarter of the butter to the pan and fry the onion for 3 minutes. Sprinkle in the garlic and rice and stir to coat well in the butter.

3 Pour in the sherry and when it has sizzled and been absorbed, add 300ml (½ pint) of the vegetable stock. Simmer and when the stock is almost absorbed, add another 300ml (½ pint) of the stock and the runner beans. Simmer for another 5 minutes and add half the remaining stock and the peppers. Stir frequently.

4 Add the rest of the stock if the rice still needs more cooking. Cook for 2–3 minutes and then push down the spinach leaves gently on top of the rice, gradually incorporating them as they wilt – about 1 minute. Don't let them wilt too much. Add chunks of the remaining butter and season well.

5 Spoon the mushrooms on top and tear the basil leaves over for garnish and extra flavour and serve.

COOK'S TIP
For a little extra creaminess, serve with Parmesan shavings.

Salmon Cabbage Parcels

These two ingredients, the humble cabbage and the ubiquitous salmon, make great partners – the sauce is rich and sharp, which elevates the whole dish.

preparation time
5 minutes

cooking time
25 minutes

310 Kcal per portion

SERVES 6

- **Spring green cabbage,** 12 whole leaves
- **Salt and freshly ground black pepper**
- **Salmon steaks,** 4 x 150g (5oz), skinned
- **Butter,** 60g (2½oz), melted
- **Fish stock,** 300ml (½ pint)
- **Butter,** 1 tbsp
- **Whipping cream,** 3 tbsp
- **Lemon juice,** 1 tbsp

1 Preheat the oven to 200°C/400°F/Gas 6. Place the cabbage leaves in a large microwave-proof dish with a small amount of water and cook in the microwave on High for 5 minutes.

2 Spread out the leaves on a tea towel, pat them dry and sprinkle with seasoning. Cut out any stiff ribs that will make it difficult to roll the leaves.

3 Cut the salmon steaks in half, horizontally. Season well and then sandwich the halves of fish together with some cabbage leaf. Wrap each steak in the remaining leaves, tucking any ends under the fish to form leaf parcels.

4 Butter a baking dish and place the parcels on it making sure the ends of the outer leaves are tucked underneath. Brush with a little butter and pour the fish stock around. Cover the dish tightly with foil.

5 Bake the fish parcels in the oven for 20 minutes. When they are cooked, pour the stock from the dish into a saucepan. Keep the fish parcels warm.

6 To make the sauce, boil the stock until slightly reduced. Reduce the heat and whisk in the butter and cream and re-heat but do not let the sauce boil. Finally, whisk in lemon juice to taste and season.

7 To serve, place the fish parcels on warm plates. Spoon the sauce around and serve. Steamed new potatoes and carrot batons would be a good accompaniment.

COOK'S TIP
To separate the leaves from the whole cabbage, cut out the core of the cabbage. Discard the tough outer leaves and pull off the remaining large leaves.

Herb-crusted Salmon

The crisp topping makes a great contrast with the silky salmon.

 preparation time
10 minutes

 cooking time
15 minutes

400 Kcal per portion

SERVES 4

- **Fresh white breadcrumbs**, 75g (3oz)
- **Parmesan cheese**, grated, 2 tbsp
- **Butter**, 25g (1oz), melted
- **Salt and freshly ground black pepper**
- **Lemon**, 1, grated zest
- **Basil or dill**, chopped, 2 tbsp
- **Salmon fillets**, 4 x 150g (5oz)

COOK'S TIP

Take care not to overcook the salmon or it will become dry – if white juices start to come out, then it's overcooked.

PLANNING AHEAD

You can make the breadcrumb topping and press it onto the salmon the night before. Cover the tray with plastic wrap and refrigerate until ready to cook.

1 Preheat the oven to 200°C/400°F/Gas 6. Mix together the breadcrumbs, Parmesan cheese, butter, seasoning, lemon zest and basil or dill.

2 Place the salmon fillets on a sheet of baking parchment on a baking tray. Divide the topping between the fillets, pressing it down quite well so that it stays on the salmon while cooking.

3 Bake in the centre of the oven for 12–15 minutes until the breadcrumb topping is golden and the salmon is just cooked. Serve at once with minted new potatoes and green beans.

Trout Fillets with Minted Cucumber

The freshness of the cucumber perfectly complements this freshwater fish.

 preparation time
10 minutes

 cooking time
15 minutes

486 Kcal per portion

SERVES 4

- **Cucumber,** ½
- **Butter,** 60g (2½oz)
- **Mint leaves,** a handful, chopped
- **Flour,** 2 tbsp
- **Salt and freshly ground black pepper**
- **Brown trout,** 4 small, filleted and skinned
- **Olive oil,** 2 tbsp
- **Crème fraîche,** 200g (7oz)

1 Peel the cucumber, slice lengthways, scoop out the seeds using a teaspoon and thinly slice. Heat a small frying pan, add half the butter and sauté the cucumber for a few minutes. Stir in a tbsp of chopped mint.

2 Put the flour onto a plate and add seasoning. Dust both sides of each trout fillet with the flour and fill each one with a quarter of the cucumber and mint.

3 Heat the remaining butter and the oil in a large frying pan and add the trout. Cook for 5–7 minutes until golden brown and crisp and then carefully turn over using 2 fish slices, one on the top and one on the bottom. Continue to cook for a further 5–7 minutes.

4 Carefully lift the fish from the pan and place on warm plates. Serve with new potatoes and sugarsnap peas (see left) accompanied by a bowl of crème fraîche mixed with the remaining chopped mint.

COOK'S TIP
While the fish is cooking, boil new potatoes, adding sugarsnap peas on top to steam covered with a lid for the last 4 minutes.

Mackerel Fish Cakes

Horseradish and peppered mackeral give these fish cakes a kick that makes them extra tasty.

**preparation time
10 minutes**

**cooking time
20 minutes**

783 Kcal per portion

SERVES 4

- **Potatoes**, 2, peeled
- **Creamed horseradish,**
  2 tbsp
- **Mayonnaise**, 4 tbsp
- **Salt and freshly ground
  black pepper**
- **Peppered smoked
  mackerel fillets,**
  350g (12oz)
- **Milk**, 2–3 tbsp
- **Butter**, 25g (1oz), melted
- **Parsley**, chopped, 1 tbsp
- **Egg**, 1, beaten
- **Fresh white breadcrumbs,**
  75g (3oz)
- **Butter**, 50g (2oz)
- **Sunflower oil**, 2 tbsp

COOK'S TIPS

If all the fish cakes will not fit in the frying pan at the same time, then cook them in two batches.

If you don't have any mashed potato, then use packet mash. If you're using left-over mashed potato, then use about 350g (12oz).

1 Cut the potatoes into 2.5cm (1in) chunks and cook in lightly salted boiling water for about 12 minutes until tender.

2 Meanwhile, stir 1 tbsp of horseradish sauce into the mayonnaise and then add seasoning.

3 Flake the mackerel fillets. Drain the potatoes well and add the milk and butter. Mash until smooth. Stir the mackerel into the mashed potato, along with the parsley and the remaining horseradish sauce. Add seasoning.

4 Divide the mixture into 8 and mould each portion into a round. Dip in egg and then coat in breadcrumbs.

5 Heat the butter and oil in a large frying pan, add the fish cakes (in batches if necessary) and cook for 4–5 minutes on each side until golden brown and heated through.

6 Serve the fish cakes, with a little of the horseradish mayonnaise spooned on top. Accompany with oven chips and a green salad.

Spicy Mackerel

This dish smells fantastic while it cooks and the avocado salad balances well with the richness of the fish.

**preparation time
15 minutes**

**cooking time
10 minutes**

488 Kcal per portion

SERVES 4

- **Onion,** 1 small, peeled and chopped
- **Garlic clove,** 1, peeled and chopped
- **Green chilli,** 1, deseeded and chopped
- **Fresh root ginger,** 2.5cm (1in) piece, peeled and chopped
- **Cumin seeds,** 1 tsp
- **Coriander,** small bunch
- **Lime,** ½, juice
- **Sugar,** pinch
- **Mackerel,** 4 gutted and cleaned, heads removed
- **Romaine or cos lettuce,** 1
- **Avocado,** 1
- **Salt and freshly ground black pepper**

1 Preheat the grill. Put the onion, garlic, chilli and ginger into a food processor and blend to make a coarse paste. Add the cumin seeds, about 3 tbsp roughly chopped coriander, the lime juice and a pinch of sugar. Blend quickly to mix.

2 Make 3 or 4 deep slashes on both sides of each mackerel and spread the spicy paste all over, pushing it into the slits and the belly. For speed and best results, use your hands.

3 Put the fish under the grill on a lightly oiled baking sheet, not too close to the heat, and cook for 4–5 minutes on each side until the skin is crispy and flesh brown.

4 Make the salad by tearing the leaves into a bowl, adding slices of peeled and stoned avocado, the rest of the lime juice and 2–3 tbsp chopped coriander leaves. Season well. Serve the mackerel with the green salad and some basmati rice.

COOK'S TIP

The fish can be cooked in a frying pan if you don't want to use the grill. Don't use a griddle as the skin may stick to the ridges that are on it.

Fry-pan Fish Supper

*This family supper in a frying pan needs no other accompaniment.
Just take it straight to the table in the frying pan and enjoy!*

**preparation time
5 minutes**

**cooking time
25 minutes**

308 Kcal per portion

SERVES 4

- **Olive oil**, 1 tbsp
- **Butter**, 15g (½oz)
- **New potatoes**, 500g (1lb 2oz), cut into 5mm (¼in) slices
- **Onion**, 1, peeled and cut into wedges
- **Plaice fillets**, 4 large, skinned
- **Salt and freshly ground black pepper**
- **Thyme sprigs**, 6
- **Tomatoes**, 4, cut into wedges
- **Green beans**, 150g (5oz), trimmed and halved
- **Lemon**, ½, cut into wedges

1 Heat a large frying pan, add the oil and butter and then the slices of potato, spreading them out in one layer if possible.

2 Pull the onion wedges apart into leaves and add to the pan. Cook for 12–15 minutes until the potatoes and onions are brown and softened, stirring every so often.

3 Put the plaice fillets, skinned side up, on the work surface and sprinkle with seasoning and thyme leaves from 2 of the sprigs. Roll them up, starting from the wide end.

4 Nestle the fish rolls into the pan among the vegetables. Put a sprig of thyme on top of each roll. Cover and cook for 5 minutes then add the wedges of tomato and cook for another 3–4 minutes.

5 Meanwhile, add the beans to a saucepan of lightly salted boiling water and cook for 4–5 minutes. Drain well and spoon into the frying pan. Add the lemon wedges, for squeezing over the fish. Serve straight from the pan.

COOK'S TIP
If you buy your fish fresh, you can ask your fishmonger to skin it for you, which will make it even quicker to cook this recipe.

VARIATION
Fillets of salmon, cod or huss or megrim (like plaice) could be used instead of plaice. Red onion or red pepper can be added at the same time as the onion, and broccoli, peas or other green vegetables can replace the beans.

Cod on a Bed of Spinach

Ginger, spring onions and soy sauce give an Oriental flavour to this healthy cod dish.

 preparation time
10 minutes

 cooking time
20 minutes

446 Kcal per portion

SERVES 4

- **Olive oil,** 5 tbsp
- **Light soy sauce,** 2 tsp
- **Cod fillets,** 4 x 200g (7oz)
- **Salt and freshly ground black pepper**
- **Spring onions,** 1 bunch, trimmed and chopped
- **Fresh root ginger,** 2cm (¾in) piece, peeled and cut into fine strips
- **Butter,** 90g (3½oz)
- **Spinach or Swiss chard,** 500g (1lb 2oz) young leaves, washed

1 Preheat the oven to 180°C/350°F/Gas 4. Mix 3 tbsp of the oil and all the soy sauce in a flat ovenproof dish and add the cod fillets. Turn them over and leave for 5 minutes and then season.

2 Heat the rest of the olive oil in a frying pan and cook the spring onions for 1–2 minutes, just to soften. Pile equally onto each piece of fish and add a few pieces of the ginger.

3 Bake in the oven for 15 minutes until the fish is cooked – the fish should be opaque in colour and when pressed with the flat of a knife should start to flake. Remove from the oven and keep warm. Pour the juices into a food processor and blend with a third of the butter. Set the sauce aside.

4 Meanwhile, heat the remaining butter in the frying pan, then add the spinach or Swiss chard and toss over the heat for about 3 minutes.

5 To serve, spoon the spinach onto warm plates, top with the cod and pour the sauce around.

COOK'S TIP
Ask the fishmonger for pieces of cod of equal thickness so that they will cook evenly. You could use haddock instead.

Smoked Haddock & Egg

The poached egg oozes into the potato making perfect comfort food.

 preparation time
15 minutes

 cooking time
15 minutes

355 Kcal per portion

SERVES 4

- **Smoked haddock,** 450g (1lb)
- **Garlic cloves, 4,** peeled and chopped
- **Thyme sprigs,** 2
- **Milk,** approximately 500ml (16fl oz) plus a little extra
- **Potatoes,** 4 large, just baked
- **Basil leaves,** a handful
- **Salt and freshly ground black pepper**
- **Eggs,** 4

1 Place the haddock in a small frying pan with the garlic and thyme and add just enough milk and water in equal quantities to cover. Bring the liquid to the boil, turn down to a simmer and cook the fish for about 10 minutes until it flakes easily when prodded.

2 Drain the fish, garlic and thyme. Remove the skin from the fish and discard it. Break up the flesh. Slice the tops off the potatoes, scoop out the soft centres and mash them in a bowl. Mix the fish, garlic and thyme with the potato. Chop most of the basil leaves and add. Season to taste and add a little milk to moisten the mash, if necessary.

3 Pile the mixture into the potato shells, making an indentation in the middle to carry the egg. Keep warm.

4 Poach the eggs in an egg poacher or bring a saucepan of water to near boiling and add a dash of vinegar. Turn down the water to a simmer, drop in the eggs and poach for 3–4 minutes until the whites set. Lift out the eggs with a slotted spoon and drain on kitchen paper.

5 To serve, place a drained hot egg on top of each potato and sprinkle with the remaining basil leaves.

COOK'S TIPS

Baked potatoes take 1 hour to cook in a hot oven or 10 minutes on High in a microwave.

To give a 'microwaved' potato a more fluffy texture, microwave it for 8 minutes and then bake it in the oven for a further 10–15 minutes to finish off.

Poached Chicken with Summer Herbs

This is a simple version of a classic French dish, full of fresh vegetables with a rich herb sauce.

 preparation time
5 minutes

 cooking time
25 minutes

386 Kcal per portion

SERVES 4

- **Boneless chicken thighs,** 4
- **Onion,** ½, peeled
- **New potatoes,** 12 small, scrubbed
- **Baby carrots,** 8
- **Salt and freshly ground black pepper**
- **Beans,** 110g (4oz), topped and tailed
- **Peas,** 50g (2oz), shelled
- **Cornflour,** 1 tbsp
- **Egg yolk,** 1
- **Butter, unsalted,** 60g (2½oz)
- **Whipping cream,** 3 tbsp
- **Parsley,** chopped, 1 tbsp
- **Chives,** chopped, 1 tbsp
- **Oregano,** chopped, 1 tbsp
- **Lemon juice,** 1 tsp

1 Place the chicken, onion, potatoes and carrot in a casserole and add cold water until the chicken and vegetables are just covered. Add salt and bring to a simmer. Cover and poach for about 20 minutes until the chicken is tender.

2 When cooked, discard the onion and lift the chicken, potatoes and carrots from the stock and keep warm. Add the beans and peas to the stock and cook for 4–5 minutes. When the vegetables are cooked, remove them from the stock and keep them warm.

3 While the vegetables are cooking, whisk the cornflour and egg yolk in a saucepan with 150ml (5fl oz) of the poaching stock. Whisk together over a low heat.

4 When the mixture begins to thicken, whisk in the butter and cream. Bring to a simmer. Add the fresh herbs and season to taste with salt, pepper and lemon juice.

5 Serve the chicken on warm plates with the vegetables and the sauce poured over.

COOK'S TIP

Don't throw away the leftover stock. Refrigerated when cool, it will keep for a few days. Otherwise freeze for later use. You may have enough stock to use for making a soup. For using in sauces at a later stage, freeze in small containers.

Marsala Chicken

The Marsala sauce tastes really special, so this chicken is perfect for midweek entertaining.

 preparation time
5 minutes

 cooking time
25 minutes

334 Kcal per portion

SERVES 4

- **Dried mixed mushrooms,** 25g (1oz)
- **Butter,** 25g (1oz)
- **Olive oil,** 1 tsp
- **Shallots,** 4, trimmed and halved or quartered, if large
- **Small cup mushrooms,** 225g (8oz), wiped
- **Chicken breasts,** 4, skinned, cut into long strips
- **Marsala,** 150ml (5fl oz)
- **Crème fraîche,** 100g (3½oz)
- **Salt and freshly ground black pepper**
- **Tarragon sprigs,** 4, to garnish

COOK'S TIP

Dried mushrooms may seem expensive but you don't need to use many to give a real flavour boost to soups, stews and sauces. If you think the soaking water looks murky, strain the mushrooms (saving the water) through a sieve lined with kitchen paper to remove any dirt. Then rinse the mushrooms in fresh water.

1 Put the dried mushrooms in a small bowl and pour over 150ml (5fl oz) hot water. Push them into the liquid and leave for 15 minutes to rehydrate.

2 Heat the butter and oil in a large frying pan and then add the shallots and cook for 5 minutes.

3 Add the cup mushrooms, stalks down, and cook until brown. Turn over and cook for another couple of minutes. Take the vegetables out of the pan with a slotted spoon and set aside.

4 Place the chicken strips in one layer in the pan. Cook, without stirring, until browned on the bottom, then turn them and cook for another few minutes. Raise the heat, pour in the Marsala and let it sizzle.

5 Return the shallots and mushrooms to the pan and let the liquid reduce for a minute or two. Pour in the rehydrated mushrooms with their soaking liquid (see Cook's tip, left). Simmer for about 5 minutes until reduced by about half.

6 Stir in the crème fraîche and warm through. Season well and garnish with tarragon leaves. Serve with mashed potatoes and green beans.

Cheesy Chicken & Mushrooms

The goat's cheese under the skin is the secret behind this moist, tasty chicken.

preparation time
5 minutes

cooking time
25 minutes

497 Kcal per portion

SERVES 4

- **Welsh goat's cheese,** 110g (4oz)
- **Chicken breasts,** 4, skin on
- **Olive oil,** 1 tbsp
- **Smoked streaky bacon rashers,** 4
- **Butter,** 25g (1oz)
- **Chestnut mushrooms,** 250g (9oz), wiped and sliced
- **Plain flour,** 1 level tbsp
- **White wine,** 250ml (8fl oz)
- **Water,** 100ml (3½ fl oz)
- **Chicken stock cube,** ½ cube, crumbled
- **Salt and freshly ground black pepper**

1 Divide the goat's cheese into 4 and push a portion under the skin of each of the chicken breasts. Heat the oil in a frying pan and when it's hot, add the chicken breasts, skin side down.

2 Cook for 4–5 minutes over a medium heat until the chicken skins are golden in colour. Turn the chicken over and cook for a further 3–4 minutes. Remove from the pan.

3 Add the bacon to the pan and cook for 2–3 minutes, then remove from the pan.

4 Add the butter to the pan and heat until foaming, then add the sliced mushrooms. Cook for 2–3 minutes until the mushrooms have started to soften, then stir in the flour.

5 Gradually stir in the wine and water, allowing the mixture to come to the boil between each addition of liquid. Stir in the crumbled stock cube.

6 Return the bacon and chicken, skin side up, to the pan and cook for a further 10–15 minutes, or until the chicken is cooked through. Season to taste before serving with mashed potatoes and green beans.

COOK'S TIPS

Take care when adding salt to this recipe – the cheese and bacon are both salty.

To save opening a large bottle of wine, look out for the small 250ml (25cl) bottles, which are perfect for this recipe.

Spicy Chicken and Saffron Rice

Quick and easy, and packed with the rich flavours and aromas of freshly-ground spices, this baked chicken is a perfect match for saffron rice.

preparation time
10 minutes

cooking time
20 minutes

600 Kcal per portion

SERVES 4

FOR THE MARINADE

- **Onion**, 1, peeled and finely chopped
- **Lemon**, 1, juice
- **Oil**, 4 tbsp
- **Salt and freshly ground black pepper**
- **Cardamom seeds**, ground, 1 tsp
- **Cinnamon**, ground, 1 tsp
- **Allspice**, ½ tsp

- **Boneless chicken breasts**, 4, skin on
- **Basmati rice**, 200g (7oz)
- **Butter**, 60g (2½oz)
- **Cinnamon stick**, ½
- **Cardamom pods**, 2, seeds roughly crushed
- **Black peppercorns**, 2, roughly crushed
- **Pistachio nuts**, 2 tbsp
- **Dried currants or blueberries**, 2 tbsp
- **Saffron threads**, a good pinch
- **Greek-style natural yogurt**, 200g (7oz), to serve

1 Preheat the oven to 180°C/350°F/Gas 4. Lightly grease a baking dish. In a bowl, whisk together all the marinade ingredients.

2 Put the chicken breasts on the baking dish and spoon the marinade over. Place in the oven for 20 minutes until cooked and golden.

3 Meanwhile, rinse the rice. Melt the butter in a deep flameproof casserole. Add the cinnamon, cardamom and pepper and stir for a few minutes before adding the drained rice, pistachios and currants or blueberries.

4 Pour enough water over the rice to cover it by 1cm (½in), season with salt and stir in the saffron threads. Bring to the boil then cover the casserole with a lid and place in the oven for 15 minutes.

5 To serve, divide the spicy rice onto 4 warmed plates and place a chicken breast on top of each. Serve with a bowl of Greek yogurt seasoned with salt and pepper.

COOK'S TIP

To grind your own spices, take 2 cardamom pods and crack using a pestle and mortar. Discard the husks and crush the remaining seeds. Then grind the peppercorns in the mortar too. If you don't have a mortar, put the pods in a plastic bag and bash them with a mallet or saucepan base.

Black Bean Duck & Noodles

Turn your kitchen into a Chinese restaurant with this easy and authentic recipe. Slices of spiced duck with plum sauce and spring onions is a classic combination.

 preparation time
5 minutes

 cooking time
25 minutes

800 Kcal per portion

SERVES 4

- **Duck breasts**, 4
- **Chinese five-spice powder**, 2 level tsp
- **Butter**, 25g (1oz)
- **Sesame oil**, 1 tbsp
- **Spring onions**, 6, trimmed and sliced
- **Root ginger**, 2.5cm (1in) piece, peeled and grated
- **Garlic clove**, 1, peeled and crushed
- **Red chilli**, 1, deseeded and sliced
- **Egg noodles**, 150g (5oz), ready cooked or straight-to-wok style
- **Sugarsnap peas**, 110g (4oz), shredded
- **Honey**, 1 tbsp
- **Dark soy sauce**, 1–2 tbsp
- **Plum sauce**, 1–2 tbsp
- **Coriander**, chopped, 2 tbsp
- **Sesame seeds**, 1 tbsp, toasted, to garnish

1 Preheat the oven to 200°C/400°F/Gas 6. Pat the duck breasts dry with kitchen paper and rub the five-spice powder into the skin.

2 Heat a large non-stick frying pan until very hot, then add the duck breasts, skin side down and cook for 5 minutes. Remove from the pan and place on a baking sheet.

3 Place the baking sheet on the top shelf of the oven and cook the duck breasts for 12–15 minutes until they are cooked to your liking. Unlike chicken, it is safe to eat duck when the meat is still pink. Take care not to over-cook the meat or it will become tough, losing its natural succulence, which is such an important part of duck's flavour.

4 Meanwhile, add the butter and sesame oil to the meat juices in the pan and heat until hot. Add the spring onions, ginger, garlic and chilli. Cook for 1–2 minutes.

5 Add the noodles and sugarsnap peas and cook until heated through. Stir in the honey and then soy sauce and plum sauce to taste.

6 Slice the duck breasts and stir into the noodles with the coriander. Serve, sprinkled with the toasted sesame seeds.

COOK'S TIP

Make sure the pan is very hot before adding the duck breasts – this helps to give a crispy skin to the duck.

Five-spice Lamb Stir-fry

*Red and Savoy cabbages add unusual colour and texture to this spicy
lamb dish sweetened with a hint of redcurrant jelly.*

 **preparation time
20 minutes**

 **cooking time
10 minutes**

298 Kcal per portion

SERVES 4

- **Leek,** 1 large
- **Red cabbage,** 225g (8oz)
- **Savoy cabbage,** 225g (8oz)
- **Lamb fillet,** 450g (1lb)
- **Chinese five-spice powder,** 1 tsp
- **Butter,** 25g (1oz)
- **Vegetable oil,** 1 tbsp
- **Garlic clove,** 1, peeled and finely chopped
- **Dark soy sauce,** 1 tbsp
- **Redcurrant jelly,** 1 tbsp
- **Chives,** chopped, 2 tbsp

1 Trim the leek and split open lengthways. Rinse under cold running water to remove any trapped earth. Shake well to remove excess water, then slice finely.

2 Discard any outer damaged leaves from the cabbages; slice out the central core and then shred the leaves very finely.

3 Trim any excess fat from the lamb, then wash the flesh and pat it dry. Cut into thin strips and season with the Chinese five-spice powder.

4 Melt the butter with the oil in a wok or large frying pan and stir-fry the garlic, lamb and leek for 5 minutes until just softened. Add the cabbage, soy sauce and redcurrant jelly, and stir-fry over a high heat for 4–5 minutes until just tender.

5 Remove from the heat and stir in the chives. Serve immediately on a bed of freshly cooked noodles or rice.

COOK'S TIP

Lamb fillet works best for this recipe as it is tender and cooks quickly. It can be a bit fatty, so trim as much fat away as you can before you cut it up.

Minted Lamb with Couscous

Based on traditional Moroccan cuisine, this lamb recipe makes a real change from plain grilled lamb steaks.

 preparation time
10 minutes

 cooking time
15 minutes

644 Kcal per portion

SERVES 4

- **Mint,** chopped, 4 tbsp
- **Balsamic vinegar,** 2 tsp
- **Salt and freshly ground black pepper**
- **Thick honey,** 4 tbsp
- **Lamb leg steaks,** 4
- **Couscous,** 225g (8oz)
- **Raisins,** 50g (2oz)
- **Water,** 450ml (¾ pint), boiling
- **Parsley,** chopped, 2 tbsp
- **Butter,** 25g (1oz), melted
- **Flaked almonds,** 25g (1oz), toasted

1 Preheat the grill to moderate heat. In a small bowl stir 2 tbsp mint, the balsamic vinegar, some seasoning and honey. Spread the mixture on all surfaces of the lamb leg steaks.

2 Place the meat on the rack of a grill pan and cook for 5–8 minutes on each side, until it is cooked to your liking and the meat starts to turn a golden colour.

3 Tip the couscous into a bowl and add the raisins. Pour over the boiling water and give the mixture a stir with a fork.

4 Leave until the grains have absorbed all the water, then stir in the remaining mint and the parsley, butter and flaked almonds and season.

5 Serve the lamb with the minty couscous, accompanied with some toasted pitta bread and shredded salad leaves.

COOK'S TIPS

To get honey off a tablespoon easily, warm the spoon under a hot tap before using it.

In place of fresh mint and balsamic vinegar use 1 tbsp of ready-bought mint sauce. If you have no fresh mint, omit it from the couscous.

Lamb with Root Vegetables

The secret to quick cooking here is in the slicing — the thinner you slice the vegetables, the faster they'll cook.

preparation time
10 minutes

cooking time
20 minutes

429 Kcal per portion

SERVES 4

- **Thyme**, chopped, 2 tbsp
- **Lamb neck fillets**, 2, trimmed
- **Salt and freshly ground black pepper**
- **Potatoes**, 250g (9oz), peeled and thinly sliced
- **Parsnips**, 250g (9oz), peeled and thinly sliced
- **Carrots**, 250g (9oz), peeled and thinly sliced
- **Olive oil**, 2–3 tbsp
- **Beetroot**, 250g (9oz), peeled and thinly sliced

COOK'S TIPS

It is important that the lamb stands for 5 minutes after coming out of the oven so that the juices can disperse in the meat.

This recipe calls for 8 minutes cooking and when the lamb comes out of the oven it will look a little pink. But don't worry. The lamb will continue cooking inside. After standing for a further 5 minutes it will be cooked to a perfect medium colour.

1 Preheat the oven to 220°C/425°F/Gas 7. Oil 3 baking trays. Massage the thyme into the meat and season to taste.

2 Mix all the sliced vegetables, except the beetroot, in a bowl and toss with salt and a little of the olive oil. Tip onto 2 of the baking trays and spread out.

3 In the same bowl toss the beetroot with salt and some more of the olive oil and place on the last baking tray. Place all the trays in the oven for about 20 minutes until slightly golden and soft to the point of a knife.

4 Meanwhile, heat a frying pan until hot, add a drop of olive oil and brown the lamb all over. Place in the oven for 8 minutes, then remove and keep warm.

5 To serve, toss the roasted root vegetables together and place on warmed plates. Slice the lamb and serve alongside. A lightly cooked green vegetable such as spinach or beans would go well with this dish.

Liver & Bacon in Mustard Gravy

An old-fashioned favourite, the flavours of liver and smoked bacon complement each other perfectly. The dish is good for you too!

preparation time
5 minutes

cooking time
25 minutes

340 Kcal per portion

SERVES 4

- **Sunflower oil**, 1 tbsp
- **Back bacon smoked rashers**, 4, de-rinded
- **Lamb's liver**, 450g (1lb), cut into 8 thin slices
- **Plain flour**, 2 level tbsp
- **Butter**, 25g (1oz)
- **Onions**, 2, peeled and sliced
- **Caster sugar**, 1 level tsp
- **Balsamic vinegar**, 1 tsp
- **Stock**, 1 lamb stock cube dissolved in 300ml (½ pint) hot water
- **Wholegrain mustard**, 1 tbsp
- **Salt and freshly ground black pepper**

COOK'S TIP

Take care not to over-cook the liver, or it will become tough.

1 Heat the oil in a frying pan and cook the bacon rashers for 2–3 minutes on each side until they start to brown. Remove them from the pan.

2 Lightly coat the slices of lamb with the flour, reserving the remaining flour. Add the lamb to the hot frying pan and cook for 30 seconds–1 minute on each side. Remove from the pan.

3 Add the butter to the pan and heat to melt. Add the onion and caster sugar and cook for 8–10 minutes until the onions have softened and are a light golden colour. Stir in the vinegar.

4 Add the remaining flour to the pan, stirring well to evenly coat the onions. Gradually stir in the stock, leaving the mixture to come to the boil between each addition of liquid, and then simmer gently for 2 minutes.

5 Stir in the mustard and season to taste. Return the bacon and liver to the pan and heat through. Serve immediately with mashed potatoes and steamed shredded cabbage.

Spicy Pork Steaks

A warming chickpea and tomato sauce makes the perfect partner to these Cajun spiced pork steaks.

 preparation time
5 minutes

 cooking time
20 minutes

527 Kcal per portion

SERVES 4

- **Olive oil**, 2 tbsp
- **Garlic cloves**, 3, peeled and chopped
- **Onion**, 1, peeled and chopped
- **Chopped tomatoes**, 400g can
- **Chickpeas**, 400g can
- **Cajun spice**, 2–3 tbsp
- **Pork steaks**, 4
- **Spinach or Swiss chard**, 350g (12oz) young leaves, washed and drained
- **Salt and freshly ground black pepper**
- **Lemon juice**, 1 tsp

1 Heat the olive oil in a frying pan and cook the garlic and onion for a few minutes to soften. Add the tomatoes. Drain the chickpeas, add to the pan and cook for 10 minutes.

2 Meanwhile, rub the Cajun spice into the pork steaks. Heat a second frying pan until really hot and dry fry the steaks for 3 minutes on each side.

3 Roughly chop the spinach or chard and stir into the tomato and bean mixture. When it has wilted, add seasoning and lemon juice.

4 Serve the vegetables on warmed deep plates with the pork steaks on top.

Pork in Creamy Apricot Sauce

The sweet fruity flavour of apricots makes this a simple supper with a difference.

preparation time
5 minutes

cooking time
15 minutes

453 Kcal per portion

SERVES 4

- **Pork tenderloin,** 450g (1lb)

- **Plain flour,** 1 tbsp

- **Salt and freshly ground black pepper**

- **Butter,** 25g (1oz)

- **Sunflower oil,** 1 tbsp

- **Apricots in fruit juice,** 411g can, puréed with the juice

- **Double cream,** 150ml (¼ pint)

- **Parsley,** chopped, to garnish

VARIATION

For something a little more special, pour 2 tbsp brandy over the pork when it's just cooked, and set it alight. This simple supper dish will then become an elegant dinner party recipe.

1 Thinly slice the pork, cutting it diagonally across the grain. Put the flour on a plate and season well. Lightly coat the slices of meat in the flour.

2 Heat the butter and oil in a large frying pan until foaming, then add the slices of pork. Cook for 3–4 minutes, until the meat is golden underneath, then turn the slices over and cook for a further 3–4 minutes, until the meat is cooked through.

3 Remove the slices of meat from the pan and keep in a dish, covered with foil, in a warm oven while making the sauce.

4 To make the sauce, add the puréed apricots to the frying pan and cook for 4–5 minutes until the quantity has reduced by about half. Add the double cream and simmer gently for 2–3 minutes until you have the desired consistency. Take care not to boil the sauce or the cream may curdle. Season to taste.

5 Arrange the meat on a warmed serving dish or individual plates and drizzle over the sauce. Garnish with parsley and serve with rice and mange tout.

Sausage Split Sandwiches

*These bacon-wrapped sausage sandwiches are perfect
for an informal supper or lunch snack.*

 **preparation time
10 minutes**

 **cooking time
15 minutes**

465 Kcal per portion

SERVES 4

- **Chipolata sausages**, 12

- **Vegetable oil**, 1 tsp

- **Streaky bacon rashers**, 6,
  de-rinded

- **Mustard, English or
  coarse-grained**, 1–2 tbsp

- **Mini-gherkins**, 6, halved
  lengthways

- **Mature Cheddar cheese**,
  50g (2oz), cut into
  12 slices

- **Bread rolls**, 4

- **Mixed salad leaves**, to
  garnish

VARIATIONS

Bigger fatter sausages can be used, too.
They'll just take 5 minutes longer to cook
and 2 per person should be enough. If
you're not keen on gherkins, leave them
out. Put ketchup in, instead of mustard, if
you prefer.

1 Preheat the grill. Brush the sausages all over with the oil and
grill them for about 10 minutes until browned all over and
cooked through.

2 Stretch each bacon rasher as long as possible with the back
of a knife, then cut it in half.

3 Split the sausages almost in half, lengthways, until they can
be opened out. Spread a little mustard inside then push in a
gherkin half and a slice of cheese.

4 Wrap half a rasher of bacon around each sausage and put
them back under the grill to cook and crisp the bacon for a
few minutes.

5 To serve, cut open the bread rolls and into each one insert a
few mixed salad leaves and 3 sausages wrapped in bacon.

Sticky Sausages & Colcannon

If it's comfort food you're after, you can't go wrong with this updated version of an Irish classic.

preparation time
10 minutes

cooking time
20 minutes

592 Kcal per portion

SERVES 4

- **Potatoes**, 680g (1lb 8oz), peeled and chopped
- **Sausages**, 8
- **Leek**, 1, trimmed, washed and finely sliced
- **Savoy cabbage**, 225g (8oz), finely shredded
- **Milk**, 6 tbsp
- **Butter**, 50g (2oz)
- **Salt and freshly ground black pepper**
- **Nutmeg**
- **Coarse-grained mustard**, 1 tbsp
- **Honey**, 1 tbsp

1 Cook the potatoes in lightly salted boiling water for 12–15 minutes until tender. Heat the grill to medium and cook the sausages for about 10 minutes until almost cooked through.

2 Drain the potatoes well, over another saucepan, so the water can be used for cooking the leek and cabbage. Bring the water to the boil, add the greens and cook for 5 minutes.

3 Put the potatoes back in the first saucepan over a low heat to dry off, then add the milk, bring to the boil, take off the heat and add 40g (1½oz) of the butter. Season well and mash until the potatoes are smooth.

4 Drain the greens well and stir them into the mash with a good sprinkling of grated nutmeg, to taste.

5 Heat the remaining butter in a frying pan and mix the mustard and honey in a small bowl. Place the sausages in the pan and spoon the mixture over the top. Cook for a few minutes, turning them, until they are cooked through, with a sticky glaze. Serve the mash in individual warm bowls, pile the sausages on top and drizzle with any extra sticky glaze.

COOK'S TIP

For fluffy mash you need floury potatoes, so look out for Maris Piper, King Edward and Desiree, or good all-rounders, Estima.

Beef Stir-fry

Have all the ingredients prepared before you start cooking; once you start creating this fresh-tasting stir-fry, you can't stop to chop or peel!

 preparation time
10 minutes

 cooking time
15 minutes

258 Kcal per portion

SERVES 4

FOR THE MARINADE

- **Dark soy sauce**, 2 tbsp
- **Sesame oil**, 2 tbsp
- **Ground coriander**, 1 tbsp
- **Brown sugar**, 1 tsp
- **Vegetable oil**, 1 tsp

- **Beef frying steak**, 200g (7oz), cut into thin strips
- **Chinese egg noodles**, 150g (5oz)
- **Onion**, ½
- **Garlic clove**, 1
- **Ginger**, 1cm (½in) piece
- **Carrot**, 1
- **Courgette**, 1
- **Mange tout**, a handful
- **Baby corn**, a handful
- **Vegetable oil**, for stir-frying
- **Lemon juice**, 1 tsp
- **Chilli**, 1, chopped (optional)
- **Sesame oil**, 1 tsp
- **Salt and freshly ground black pepper**
- **Coriander leaves**, a handful, to garnish

1 Mix the marinade ingredients together in a bowl. Stir in the meat and leave to marinate while you prepare the other ingredients. Soak the noodles in boiling water for 5 minutes, then drain.

2 Meanwhile, peel and slice the onion and garlic; peel and grate the ginger; peel the carrot and cut into finger pieces together with the courgette, and top and tail the mange tout.

3 Heat the wok until smoking hot. Add 2 tbsp of vegetable oil, then add the onion, garlic and ginger. Stir the ingredients by lifting and moving them with a wooden spatula. You can also shake the wok to keep the food moving.

4 Drain the meat and reserve the marinade, push the onion mixture up the sides of the wok and fry the beef in batches, pushing the cooked pieces up the wok side as you add the rest. Tip the meat and onions into a bowl.

5 Add a little more oil to the wok. Add the carrot and then the courgette, stirring constantly for about 4 minutes until partly cooked.

6 Add the corn, the mange tout and the drained noodles, tossing and stirring all the time. Finally return the beef and onions to the wok to heat through. Bring the marinade to the boil in a small saucepan.

7 Season to taste with a little of the marinade (discarding the rest) and the lemon juice, chopped chilli (if liked) and sesame oil. Add seasoning, sprinkle with torn coriander leaves and serve immediately.

COOK'S TIP

When you are looking for frying steak, top end of rump is a good cut to choose.

Beef & Horseradish Burgers

Enjoy a take-away at home with these burgers with a difference – the horseradish gives an extra unexpected kick to an otherwise traditional recipe.

 preparation time
15 minutes

 cooking time
10 minutes

354 Kcal per portion

SERVES 4

- **Minced beef**, 450g (1lb)
- **Fresh white breadcrumbs**, 50g (2oz)
- **Creamed horseradish**, 1 tbsp
- **Parsley**, chopped, 2 tbsp
- **Salt and freshly ground black pepper**
- **Sunflower oil**, 2–3 tbsp

COOK'S TIP

If you want the burgers all to be exactly the same shape, shape them inside a plain round pastry cutter.

1 Place the beef in a bowl and add the breadcrumbs, horseradish sauce and parsley and season well. Mix the ingredients together well.

2 Divide the beef mixture into 8, and shape each portion into a burger. Place the burgers on a board and chill for 5 minutes before cooking.

3 Heat the oil in a large frying pan and add the burgers. Cook for 4–5 minutes on each side, or until cooked through. Serve immediately in bread rolls with slices of tomato, gherkin and a few onion rings.

Beef in a Bun

This recipe is a bit of fun. Spoil yourself with some fillet of beef and remember it is important not to overcook the beef unless you like it well done.

 preparation time
10 minutes

 cooking time
15 minutes

499 Kcal per portion

SERVES 4

- **Bread,** 8 slices country-style loaf
- **Sesame seeds**
- **Butter,** 60g (2½oz)
- **Olive oil,** 1 tbsp
- **Onions,** 2, peeled and chopped
- **Mushrooms,** 8, wiped and quartered
- **Beef, fillet or rib eye,** 450g (1lb), cubed
- **Salt and freshly ground black pepper**
- **Dark soy sauce,** 1–2 tbsp
- **Water,** 125ml (4fl oz)

COOK'S TIP
Rosti rings are like biscuit cutters, but without the sharp edges. They can be used for assembling hot and cold, cooked and uncooked recipes. They usually measure 8–9cm (3¼–3½in) diameter and 4–5cm (1½–2in) in height. They give a neat, professional presentation.

1 Preheat the oven to 180°C/350°F/Gas 4. Cut the bread into circles to fit 4 rosti rings. Mix the sesame seeds with the butter and spread on one side of each slice.

2 Heat the oil in a frying pan until hot and then add the onions and mushrooms. Cook for 5 minutes until partially done, then tip into a large bowl. Get the pan really hot again and add the beef. Cook for 1 minute, turning the meat once. Tip the beef into the bowl of mushrooms and season.

3 Add the soy sauce to the pan with the water to deglaze it. Cook for another minute and then pour the juices into the bowl and mix the ingredients thoroughly.

4 Put the rosti rings on a baking sheet and, into each one, put a bread circle, buttered side down. Pile in the beef mixture and press with a spoon. Put the remaining slices on top, buttered side up. Place the tray in the oven for 2–3 minutes to reheat.

5 To serve, remove the tray from the oven and transfer the 'buns' to warm plates. Lift the (hot) ring off each plate. Accompany with a salad.

Glazed Sirloin Steak with Chips

With this juicy steak and crisp oven-baked chips you can have a restaurant-style meal at home in just 30 minutes – and for a fraction of the price!

**preparation time
5 minutes**

**cooking time
25 minutes**

357 Kcal per portion

SERVES 4

- **Potatoes**, 680g (1lb 8oz), peeled
- **Olive oil**, 2 tbsp
- **Butter**, 15g (½oz)
- **Onion**, 1, peeled and sliced
- **Thin cut sirloin steaks**, 4
- **Redcurrant jelly**, 2 tbsp
- **Balsamic vinegar**, 2 tbsp
- **Rosemary**, chopped, 1 tsp

1 Preheat the oven to 220°C/425°F/Gas 7 and put in a large baking sheet to heat. Cut the potatoes into 5mm (¼in) slices and parboil in a saucepan of lightly salted boiling water for about 10 minutes.

2 Meanwhile, heat 1 tsp of the oil with the butter and fry the onion over a low to medium heat for about 10 minutes until softened and lightly browned.

3 Drain the potatoes well, reserving some of the liquid. Sprinkle a little oil onto the hot baking sheet, spread the potatoes over in one layer and sprinkle with more oil. Cook the potatoes in the oven for 15 minutes, turning them once, until lightly browned and crisp.

4 Meanwhile, take the onions out of the saucepan with a slotted spoon and set aside, keeping them warm. Heat the pan again, add the steaks, cooking 2 at a time, for 2 minutes on each side. Remove the steaks from the pan and keep them warm.

5 Spoon the jelly, balsamic vinegar and rosemary into the pan with 2 tbsp of the reserved potato cooking water. Stir the sauce until the jelly dissolves and the sauce reduces and thickens a little.

6 Arrange the potatoes on 4 warmed plates and garnish each with the fried onions. Then put a steak on each plate and spoon over the sauce.

Beef & Shallot Stew

A simple stew – if you buy the quantity of beef that you need, you won't need scales for the other ingredients (just a measuring jug for the liquids) – it's cooking by numbers!

preparation time
5 minutes

cooking time
25 minutes

399 Kcal per portion

SERVES 4

- **Sunflower oil**, 2 tbsp
- **Scotch beef frying steak**, 450g (1lb), cubed
- **Shallots**, 12
- **Celery**, 2 sticks
- **Carrots**, 2
- **Parsnips**, 2
- **Unsalted butter**, 25g (1oz)
- **Plain flour**, 2 tbsp
- **Red wine**, 300ml (½ pint)
- **Beef stock**, 300ml (½ pint)
- **Gravy browning**, dash (optional)
- **Thyme**, chopped, 1 tbsp
- **Salt and freshly ground black pepper**

FREEZING

To freeze, pack into a freezer container, seal and freeze for up to 3 months. Allow to defrost in a cool place before re-heating.

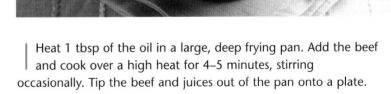

1 Heat 1 tbsp of the oil in a large, deep frying pan. Add the beef and cook over a high heat for 4–5 minutes, stirring occasionally. Tip the beef and juices out of the pan onto a plate.

2 Meanwhile, prepare the vegetables: peel the shallots, slice the celery sticks and peel and slice the carrots and parsnips.

3 Heat the butter and remaining oil in the pan and add the vegetables. Cook for about 5 minutes until they start to soften.

4 Add the flour to the pan and stir into the juices, then gradually add the red wine and beef stock, allowing the mixture to come to the boil between each addition of liquid.

5 Return the beef and juices to the pan and stir in a little gravy browning, if liked. Stir in the thyme and season to taste.

6 Cover the pan and simmer for 15–20 minutes until the vegetables and meat are just tender. Serve immediately with mashed potato or potato croquettes, and peas.

Casseroles & Bakes

For times when you want to cook now and eat later,

try one of these delicious dishes. Even old favourites

like Lasagne (p 121) or Lancashire Hot Pot (p 110)

take less than 30 minutes work in the kitchen.

While they bake, you can get on with something else,

or even put your feet up! If you use a flameproof

casserole, you can transfer it from hob to oven to table,

saving on washing up as well as time.

Leek Gratin with Olive Relish

Black olives and fresh tomatoes are a zingy combination to accompany the leek gratin.

 preparation time
20 minutes

 cooking time
20 minutes

520 Kcal per portion
Suitable for vegetarians

SERVES 4

- **Leek**, 1
- **Parsnips**, 350g (12oz), peeled
- **Parmesan cheese**, 75g (3oz)
- **Eggs**, 3
- **Double or whipping cream**, 60ml (2fl oz)
- **Salt and freshly ground black pepper**
- **Thyme**, chopped, 1 tbsp

FOR THE RELISH

- **Olive oil**, 6 tbsp
- **Garlic cloves**, 4, peeled and halved
- **Red onions**, 2, peeled and cut into wedges
- **Black olives**, 50g (2oz)
- **Balsamic vinegar**, 2 tsp
- **Vegetable stock**, 60ml (2fl oz)
- **Tomatoes**, 4, quartered

1 Preheat the oven to 180°C/350°F/Gas 4. Grease a gratin dish. Clean the leek. Cut the leek and parsnips in half lengthways.

2 Bring a saucepan of lightly salted water to the boil. Add the leeks and parsnips and cook for 5 minutes until partly cooked. Drain the vegetables.

3 Put the Parmesan in a food processor and chop. Then add the eggs and cream and blend. Add seasoning.

4 Sprinkle the base of the gratin dish with some of the thyme and cover with a layer of parsnips and leeks. Pour over a thin layer of the egg mixture and continue layering. Bake in the oven for about 20 minutes until the vegetables are tender and the egg is set. Serve the gratin from the dish with the following relish.

5 For the relish, heat 2 tbsp of the oil in a saucepan and cook the garlic and onion wedges for a few minutes until softening. Add the olives, balsamic vinegar and stock.

6 Cover with a lid and simmer for 15–20 minutes until the onions are tender. Add the tomatoes and heat through. Check seasoning and add the remaining olive oil.

Stilton & Garlic Bread Bake

That old favourite, bread and butter pudding, is given a savoury twist with Stilton.

 preparation time
25 minutes

 cooking time
25 minutes

495 Kcal per portion

SERVES 4

- **Garlic ciabatta**, 2 x 260g ready-made chilled loaves
- **Smoked streaky bacon rashers**, 4, grilled and chopped
- **Eggs**, 3
- **Milk**, 600ml (1 pint)
- **Freshly ground black pepper**
- **Stilton cheese**, 110g (4oz)

1 Preheat the oven to 200°C/ 400°F/Gas 6. Separate the slices of bread and arrange, overlapping, in an ovenproof dish. Sprinkle over the bacon.

2 Beat together the eggs, milk and pepper and pour over the bread. Leave to stand for about 5 minutes, for the egg mixture to soak into the bread.

3 Sprinkle over the Stilton cheese. Bake in the centre of the oven for 20–25 minutes, until a light golden colour on top. Serve immediately with tomato salad.

COOK'S TIPS
Take care over the seasoning of this dish – don't add any extra salt as there is enough saltiness from the bacon and cheese.

If you can't find ready-made chilled garlic ciabattas, then make your own by spreading some garlic butter over a sliced ciabatta loaf. Ordinary garlic bread can also be used – if it's frozen, allow to defrost so that you can separate the slices.

VARIATION
For a vegetarian version, omit the bacon or use a vegetarian bacon substitute.

Spanakopitta

A Greek speciality, this delicious spinach pie can be served hot or cold.

**preparation time
25 minutes**

**cooking time
45 minutes**

630 Kcal per portion
Suitable for vegetarians

SERVES 4

- **Leeks**, 450g (1lb)
- **Spring onions**, 1 bunch
- **Butter**, 110g (4oz)
- **Olive oil**, 1 tbsp
- **Baby spinach leaves**,
  2 x 250g bags
- **Eggs**, 3 large
- **Single cream**, 250ml
  (8fl oz)
- **Feta cheese**, 200g pack
- **Freshly ground black
  pepper**
- **Nutmeg**
- **Filo pastry**, 200g (7oz)

1 Preheat the oven to 200°C/400°F/Gas 6. Grease a shallow non-stick baking tin measuring 28 x 18cm (11 x 7in).

2 Trim, wash and slice the leeks and spring onions. Heat 25g (1oz) of the butter and the oil in a large frying pan.

3 Add the leeks and spring onions and cook until softened, but not browned. Add the spinach (half at a time if necessary) and continue cooking until the spinach is wilted. Then increase the heat and bubble off excess liquid and remove from heat.

4 In a large bowl, whisk together the eggs and cream. Crumble the feta cheese into the bowl, add the spinach mixture and season well with black pepper and freshly grated nutmeg.

5 Melt the remaining butter in a saucepan. Brush 3 sheets of filo with the butter and arrange across the baking tin so the bottom is covered and the excess overhangs the sides and ends.

6 Using 6 more sheets of filo, repeat step 5 twice more. Take one more sheet of filo, brush with butter and place it lengthways along the bottom.

7 Pour the spinach filling into the lined tin. Brush another sheet of filo and place it lengthways, buttered side down, on top of the filling, then brush the top side with butter. Brush and add two more sheets of filo.

8 Fold the overhanging filo pastry over the top of the pie, slightly rouching it as you do so. Finally, brush the last sheet of filo with butter and place it down the centre, gently rouching it to match the sides. Brush any remaining butter over the top.

9 Bake for 45 minutes until it is golden brown and the filling is set. If necessary, cover the top of the pie with a sheet of foil to prevent it over-browning. The pie should feel firm and springy to the touch and a skewer inserted into the centre should come out clean.

10 Allow the pie to cool a little before cutting it into squares for serving. Tomato and olive salad makes a good accompaniment.

COOK'S TIPS

You can buy filo pastry in most supermarkets – either fresh from the chiller cabinet or frozen.

As feta cheese is quite salty it shouldn't be necessary to add any more salt when seasoning this dish.

Potato Pie

Layers of thinly sliced potato and colourful sweet peppers make this a filling and tasty dish fit for a winter's evening.

 preparation time
25 minutes

 cooking time
40 minutes

555 Kcal per portion
Suitable for vegetarians

SERVES 4

- **Potatoes**, 1.3kg (3lb)
- **Salt and freshly ground black pepper**
- **Red peppers**, 2
- **Green peppers**, 2
- **Butter**, 50g (2oz)
- **Light olive oil**, 2 tbsp
- **Milk**, 2–3 tbsp
- **Chives**, chopped, 5 tbsp
- **Mature Cheddar cheese**, grated, 200g (7oz)

PLANNING AHEAD

This pie can be made well in advance, even the day before, and kept, covered, in the refrigerator.

1 Peel the potatoes and cut them into 5mm (¼in) thick slices to help speed up the cooking. At the same time bring a kettle of water to the boil.

2 Place the potatoes in a large saucepan, add 1 tsp of salt, cover with boiling water and cook for 10–15 minutes until tender. Preheat the oven to 200°C/400°F/Gas 6.

3 Meanwhile, core, deseed and thinly slice the peppers. Heat 25g (1oz) of the butter and the oil in a large frying pan. Add the peppers and cook for about 10 minutes until softened, stirring frequently.

4 Drain the cooked potatoes, then mash with the milk and the remaining butter. Season well and beat in the chives and three-quarters of the cheese.

5 Evenly spread half of the potato mixture in an ovenproof dish. Top with the peppers, then cover with remaining potatoes and spread evenly. Mark the top of the pie into swirls and sprinkle with the remaining cheese.

6 Bake in the oven for 35–40 minutes until golden brown. Serve with a tossed green salad or cold meats.

Macaroni Cheese

Deliciously cheesy, this macaroni cheese is the ultimate comfort food.

preparation time
10 minutes

cooking time
35 minutes

651 Kcal per portion
Suitable for vegetarians

SERVES 4

- **Mature Cheddar cheese,** 75g (3oz)
- **Double Gloucester cheese,** 75g (3oz)
- **Lancashire cheese,** 75g (3oz)
- **Spring onions,** 1 bunch
- **Fresh pasta, spirals or penne,** 500g (1lb 2oz)
- **Butter,** 25g (1oz)
- **Plain flour,** 3 tbsp
- **Milk,** 600ml (1 pint)
- **Wholegrain mustard,** ½ tbsp
- **Salt and freshly ground black pepper**

VARIATION

If preferred, you can use just one type of cheese or any other mixture according to what you may have in the refrigerator. Just ensure that you use a total of 225g (8oz).

1 Preheat the oven to 200°C/400°F/Gas 6. Put a large saucepan of lightly salted water on to boil.

2 Coarsely grate the cheeses and mix them together. Trim, wash and thinly slice the spring onions. Add the pasta to the boiling water and cook as directed on the packet.

3 Meanwhile, melt the butter in a large saucepan, add the spring onions and cook for 2–3 minutes until softened. Then stir in the flour.

4 Add the milk and bring to the boil, stirring constantly. Stir the mustard and three-quarters of the cheese into the sauce, stirring until all the cheese is melted. Add seasoning.

5 Drain the pasta and mix into the cheese sauce. Then pour into a large ovenproof dish and scatter the top with the remaining cheese.

6 Place the dish on a baking tray and bake for 20–25 minutes until golden brown. Serve immediately with a tomato and red onion salad.

Mexican Eggs

Hot, spicy, Mexican-style chilli sauce adds a Latin touch to this meal-in-a-dish.

 preparation time
25 minutes

 cooking time
30 minutes

560 Kcal per portion
Suitable for vegetarians

SERVES 4

- **Potatoes**, 1.3kg (3lb)
- **Salt and freshly ground black pepper**
- **Butter**, 75g (3oz)
- **Baby spinach leaves**, 500g (1lb 2oz)
- **Nutmeg**
- **Single cream**, 3–4 tbsp
- **Milk**, 3 tbsp
- **Eggs**, 4 large
- **Tomato and chilli sauce**, 200g jar
- **Cheddar cheese**, 75g (3oz)

VARIATION
For a milder taste, use a fresh tomato sauce.

PLANNING AHEAD
The potato and spinach layers of this dish can be prepared in advance and kept, covered, in the refrigerator until ready to bake.

1 Peel the potatoes and cut them into thick slices. At the same time bring a kettle of water to the boil.

2 Place the potatoes in a large saucepan, add 1 tsp of salt, cover with boiling water and cook for 10–15 minutes until tender. Preheat the oven to 200°C/400°F/Gas 6.

3 Meanwhile, melt half of the butter in a large saucepan, add the spinach and stir-fry until wilted. Off the heat, season and add freshly grated nutmeg. Stir in the cream and set aside.

4 Drain the potatoes, season and mash with the milk and remaining butter. Spread in a shallow ovenproof dish and smooth the top. Spread the spinach over the potatoes.

5 With a small ramekin dish make four evenly spaced large hollows in the spinach large enough to hold 1 egg.

6 One at a time, crack open the eggs and drop them into the hollows in the spinach. Spoon the tomato and chilli sauce over and around the eggs and grate the cheese over the top.

7 Bake in the oven for 10–15 minutes until the dish is piping hot and the eggs are set.

Tuna Noodle Bake

Dill and capers add a little extra to that excellent standby, the can of tuna.

 preparation time
20 minutes

 cooking time
40 minutes

529 Kcal per portion

SERVES 4

- **Red onion**, 1
- **Cup mushrooms**, 350g (12oz)
- **Butter**, 75g (3oz)
- **Salt and freshly ground black pepper**
- **Fresh tagliatelle**, 250g (9oz)
- **Plain flour**, 3 tbsp
- **Milk**, 600ml (1 pint)
- **Tuna**, in brine, 2 x 200g cans
- **Capers**, 2–3 tbsp
- **Fresh dill**, 25g pack, plus a little extra, for garnish
- **Parmesan cheese**, 50g (2oz)

1 Preheat the oven to 200°C/400°F/Gas 6. Put a large saucepan of lightly salted water on to boil.

2 Peel and thinly slice the onion; wipe, trim and quarter the mushrooms. Melt 50g (2oz) of the butter in a large frying pan, add the onion and cook until slightly softened. Then add the mushrooms and cook until lightly browned, always stirring.

3 As soon as the water comes to the boil, add 1 tsp salt and the pasta and cook as directed on the packet. Then drain well and return to the saucepan.

4 Meanwhile, melt the remaining butter in a saucepan, stir in the flour and then slowly add the milk, stirring constantly. Bring to the boil.

5 Drain and flake the tuna and stir into the white sauce together with the onion and mushroom mixture, capers and dill. Add seasoning to taste.

6 Pour the sauce over the pasta, mix gently and pour into a large, shallow, ovenproof dish. Grate the Parmesan and sprinkle it evenly over the top of the pasta.

7 Place the baking dish on a baking tray and cook in the oven for 20–25 minutes until the top is golden brown. Garnish with dill and serve immediately with a mixed leaf or rocket salad.

COOK'S TIPS

A few drops of oil added to the water will help prevent the water boiling over.

To help prevent getting lumps in the white sauce, add all the ingredients and then whisk until they come to the boil.

Salmon & Prawn Pie

This pie looks really special but is so easy to make that it's ideal for a quick supper.

preparation time
25 minutes

cooking time
25 minutes

582 Kcal per portion

SERVES 4

- **Salmon fillet**, 250g (9oz)
- **Crème fraîche**, 200g (7oz)
- **Soft cheese with garlic and herbs**, 110g (4oz)
- **Eggs**, 2
- **Dill or chives**, chopped, 2 tbsp
- **Salt and freshly ground black pepper**
- **Prawns**, 110g (4oz) cooked, defrosted if frozen
- **Filo pastry**, 4 sheets approximately 38 x 28cm (15 x 11in)
- **Butter**, 25–50g (1–2oz), melted

1 Preheat the oven to 200°C/400°F/Gas 6 and place a baking sheet in the oven to heat up. Bring a medium-sized saucepan of water to the boil.

2 Cut the salmon into 2cm (¾in) cubes and add to the water. Allow the water to come to the boil again, then remove the pan from the heat. Leave the salmon to poach for 3–4 minutes, then drain well and leave it to cool slightly.

3 Mix together the crème fraîche, soft cheese, eggs, chopped herbs and add plenty of seasoning. Carefully fold in the prawns and the salmon, until mixed, but taking care so that the fish does not break up.

4 Cut each sheet of filo pastry into a square, reserving the ends that are cut off. Brush one square with butter and place another square on top – twisting it so that it does not line up with the first one – and brush with butter.

5 Repeat with the remaining 2 squares, twisting each one so they spiral around and all the points are evenly spread out. Lift into a fluted flan tin (23cm/9in diameter), leaving the excess hanging over the edge.

6 Spoon in the filling, levelling the surface. Scrunch in the ends of the pastry so they partially cover the filling.

7 Brush the last trimmings of pastry with butter, and cut into long thin strips. Crumple these strips over the rim of the pie.

8 Place the pie on the hot baking sheet and bake towards the top of the oven for 20–25 minutes until the pastry is crisp and golden and the filling is set. Serve the pie either warm or cold and with a green salad.

COOK'S TIPS

Remove the pie from the oven when the filling is only just set – if you cook it for too long, the filling will curdle.

If you have a microwave oven, place the salmon cubes on a plate. Partially cover with all-purpose cling film and cook on high power for 2½–3½ minutes, or until the salmon is just cooked. Drain the juices before using the salmon.

Coriander Chicken Casserole

Earthy coriander leaves and sweet creamed coconut combine to make chicken special.

 preparation time
20 minutes

 cooking time
1½ hours

552 Kcal per portion

SERVES 4

- **Butter,** 25g (1oz)
- **Olive oil,** 1 tbsp
- **Chicken thighs and legs,** 4 of each, skin on
- **Onions,** 2, peeled and chopped
- **Garlic cloves,** 2, peeled and crushed
- **Coriander,** ground, 2 tsp
- **Flour,** 1 tbsp
- **Chicken stock,** 600ml (1 pint)
- **Fine green beans,** 450g (1lb), trimmed
- **Creamed coconut,** 25g (1oz)
- **Salt and freshly ground black pepper**
- **Coriander,** chopped, 5 tbsp

1 Preheat the oven to 180°C/350°F/Gas 4. Heat the butter and oil in a large flameproof casserole. Pat the chicken pieces dry with kitchen paper, add to the casserole and brown lightly all over. Remove from the casserole and set aside.

2 Add the onion and garlic to the casserole and cook until slightly softened. Stir in the ground coriander and flour, then add the stock and bring to the boil, stirring to smooth out any lumps. Add the beans and coconut and season well.

3 Return the chicken pieces to the casserole and coat with the sauce. Cover with a sheet of greaseproof paper to prevent excess evaporation, then cover with a lid or foil and cook in the oven for about 1½ hours until the chicken is very tender.

4 Stir the fresh coriander into the casserole and serve with warm naan bread or rice.

COOK'S TIP

Chicken thighs and drumsticks can be bought together, ready prepared and pre-packed. Alternatively, use a whole chicken and joint it yourself.

Rice with Everything

Chorizo sausage, Serrano ham and pimento slices give this dish a truly Spanish flavour.

 preparation time
15 minutes

 cooking time
40 minutes

767 Kcal per portion

SERVES 4

- **Olive oil,** 4 tbsp
- **Boneless chicken breasts,** 300g (11oz), skinned and chopped
- **Chorizo sausage,** 70g (2½oz), sliced
- **Boneless pork,** 110g (4oz), diced
- **Serrano ham slices,** 70g (2½oz)
- **Garlic cloves,** 2, peeled and finely chopped
- **Chicken livers,** 2, cleaned and quartered
- **Paella or risotto rice,** 400g (14oz), rinsed
- **Paprika,** 1 tsp
- **Cayenne pepper,** a pinch
- **Passata sauce,** 3 tbsp
- **Salt and freshly ground black pepper**
- **Chicken stock,** 1.2 litres (2 pints)
- **Dry white wine,** 200ml (7fl oz)
- **Frozen peas,** 110g (4oz)
- **Pimentos (red peppers in a jar),** 2, cut into strips
- **Egg,** 1, hard boiled and sliced
- **Parsley,** chopped, 2 tbsp

1 Heat the oil in a large saucepan and cook the chicken and chorizo until browned. Add the pork and Serrano ham and cook until browned and then add the garlic and livers.

2 Add the rice, paprika, cayenne pepper and passata. Season and stir well.

3 Add half the stock with the wine. When the liquid has been absorbed, add the remaining stock and frozen peas. Cover with a lid and cook on the hob for 20–25 minutes until all the liquid is absorbed and the rice is done.

4 Decorate the top with the pimento, hard-boiled egg and parsley. Cover the pan and stand for 5 minutes in a warm place by the cooker so that the rice grains separate.

COOK'S TIPS

If you have a fresh pepper, halve and grill it until the skin blisters and use it instead of pimento.

Italian passata is available in jars and cartons in most supermarkets.

Normandy Chicken Casserole

A free-range, corn-fed chicken will give this casserole a richer, more full-bodied flavour – but it is by no means essential.

 preparation time
25 minutes

 cooking time
2 hours

702 Kcal per portion

SERVES 6

- **Corn-fed chicken**, 2.25kg (5lb)
- **Plain flour**, 2 tbsp
- **Salt and freshly ground black pepper**
- **Butter**, 25g (1oz)
- **Olive oil**, 1 tbsp
- **Onions**, 2
- **Baby carrots**, 250g (9oz)
- **Baby new potatoes**, 450g (1lb)
- **Lean, rindless back bacon rashers**, 150g (5oz)
- **Button mushrooms**, 400g (14oz)
- **Chicken stock**, 600ml (1 pint)
- **Dry white wine**, 300ml (½ pint)
- **Tarragon**, 25g (1oz) packet
- **Single cream**, 150ml (¼ pint)

COOK'S TIP

It is cheaper to buy a whole chicken and cut it into joints yourself but if you can't find a corn-fed chicken, buy a pre-cut pack of chicken pieces – 2kg (4lb 8oz). If jointing a chicken, cut away the backbone after removing the leg and thigh joints. This will not be needed for the casserole, but can be kept for making a delicious stock.

1 Preheat the oven to 180°C/350°F/Gas 4. If using a whole chicken, cut it into 8 portions (2 legs, 2 thighs, 4 pieces of breast), discarding the backbone. Rinse the pieces and pat them dry with kitchen paper.

2 Put the flour onto a large plate and season well, then lightly coat the chicken pieces with the flour, shaking off the excess.

3 Heat the butter and oil in a large flameproof casserole, add the chicken pieces in a single layer (half at a time if necessary) and lightly brown all over. Remove and set aside.

4 Meanwhile, peel and cut the onions in half, then cut each half into three. Rinse and dry the carrots and potatoes, cut the bacon into wide strips and wipe the mushrooms.

5 Add the onions, carrots and bacon to the fat remaining in the casserole and cook for 3–4 minutes until the onions are lightly browned. Then stir in the stock and wine and bring to the boil, stirring constantly.

6 Return the chicken to the casserole, add the potatoes and half of the tarragon sprigs. Cover the surface with greaseproof paper to

prevent excess evaporation, then cover with a lid or foil and cook in the oven for about 2 hours until the chicken is very tender.

7 Just before serving, remove the leaves from the remaining tarragon sprigs. Stir the cream into the casserole, season well with freshly ground black pepper and scatter the tarragon leaves over the surface.

Chicken Cobbler

Savoury cheese and herb scones make an unusual topping to creamy chicken with corn.

 preparation time
30 minutes

 cooking time
35 minutes

849 Kcal per portion

SERVES 4

- **Butter,** 40g (1½oz)
- **Chicken strips,** 550g (1lb 4oz)
- **Plain flour,** 4 tbsp
- **Chicken stock,** 425ml (¾ pint)
- **Single cream,** 150ml (¼ pint)
- **Sweetcorn,** frozen, 200g (7oz)
- **Salt and freshly ground black pepper**

FOR THE SCONES

- **Self-raising flour,** 225g (8oz)
- **Baking powder,** ¼ tsp
- **Salt**
- **Mixed dried herbs,** 1 tsp
- **Butter,** 50g (2oz), at room temperature
- **Mature Cheddar cheese,** 150g (5oz), grated
- **Egg,** 1 large
- **Milk,** for mixing

1 Preheat the oven to 220°C/425°F/Gas 7. Lightly butter a 25cm (10in) diameter shallow ovenproof dish.

2 Melt the butter in a large frying pan until bubbling hot, add the chicken strips and stir-fry until lightly browned.

3 Stir the flour into the chicken, then add the stock and bring to the boil, stirring constantly. Remove from the heat and stir in the cream and sweetcorn. Season well, pour into the ovenproof dish, level the surface and set aside.

4 To make the scones, sift the flour, baking powder and a good pinch of salt into a mixing bowl. Stir in the herbs, add the butter and rub in until the mixture resembles fine breadcrumbs.

5 Mix three-quarters of the cheese into the rubbed-in mixture and make a well in the centre. Beat the egg and make it up to 150ml (¼ pint) with milk. Pour into the flour and mix to form a fairly soft dough.

6 Turn onto a floured surface, knead lightly until smooth, then roll out to approximately 1cm (½in) thick. Using a 6cm (2½in) diameter plain round cutter, stamp out rounds from the dough and set aside.

7 Re-knead and re-roll trimmings and stamp out more rounds until you have used all the dough.

8 Arrange the scones evenly on top of the chicken mixture, around the edge of the dish, brush with a little milk and sprinkle with the remaining cheese.

9 Bake in the oven for about 30–35 minutes until the scones are well risen, golden brown and firm to the touch. Serve with a green salad.

COOK'S TIP

Ready-prepared chicken strips can be found in most supermarkets. But if you can't find them or they are too pricey, buy chicken breasts, skin them and cut into strips instead.

Chicken & Prawn Jambalaya

A New Orleans speciality, this oven-cooked jambalaya is completely hassle free.

preparation time
20 minutes

cooking time
1½ hours

650 Kcal per portion

SERVES 6

- **Chicken thighs**, 8, skin on
- **Salt and freshly ground black pepper**
- **Butter**, 25g (1oz)
- **Olive oil**, 2 tbsp
- **Onions**, 2
- **Garlic cloves**, 2
- **Green pepper**, 1 large
- **Red pepper**, 1 large
- **Pepperoni sausage**, 200g (7oz)
- **Long grain rice**, 225g (8oz)
- **Chopped tomatoes**, 400g can
- **Mixed dried herbs**, 1 tbsp
- **Chicken stock**, 600ml (1 pint)
- **Frozen peas**, 225g (8oz)
- **Frozen peeled prawns**, 200g (7oz), thawed
- **Parsley**, chopped, 4 tbsp

1 Preheat the oven to 180°C/350°F/Gas 4. Pat the chicken thighs dry with kitchen paper and season well.

2 Heat the butter and olive oil in a large flameproof casserole until sizzling, then add the chicken thighs and brown lightly all over. Remove from the casserole and set aside.

3 Meanwhile, peel and chop the onions and peel and crush the garlic. Then core, deseed and slice the peppers and thickly slice the pepperoni.

4 Add the onions, garlic and peppers to the casserole and cook for 3–4 minutes until slightly softened, stirring frequently.

5 Add the pepperoni, rice, tomatoes, herbs and stock and bring to the boil. Return the chicken to the casserole, add the peas and mix well together.

6 Cover the casserole with a tightly fitting lid and cook in the oven for 1¼–1½ hours until the chicken thighs are tender, the rice is cooked and all the liquid has been absorbed.

7 Scatter the thawed prawns, which are small and will heat up on contact with this steaming dish, together with the parsley over the jambalaya and serve with a tossed green salad.

COOK'S TIP

A wire mesh splatter guard is invaluable, especially when browning chicken. You can buy one quite cheaply from most kitchenware shops and departments.

Turkey Goujons with Thyme

This rich and creamy one-dish meal is elegant enough for entertaining.

 preparation time
25 minutes

 cooking time
45 minutes

517 Kcal per portion

SERVES 4

- **Asparagus tips**, 100g (3½oz)
- **Leeks**, 2
- **Onion**, 1 large
- **Courgettes**, 400g (14oz)
- **Butter**, 25g (1oz)
- **Olive oil**, 2 tbsp
- **Turkey strips**, 550g (1lb 4oz)
- **Plain flour**, 3 tbsp
- **White wine**, 150ml (¼ pint)
- **Chicken stock**, 300ml (½ pint)
- **Thyme leaves**, chopped, 2 tbsp
- **Single cream**, 150ml (¼ pint)
- **Salt and freshly ground black pepper**
- **Fresh white breadcrumbs**, 9 tbsp
- **Parmesan cheese**, grated, 3 tbsp

1 Preheat the oven to 200°C/400°F/Gas 6. Bring a small saucepan of water to the boil, add the asparagus tips and cook for 2–3 minutes until just softened. Pour into a colander, rinse and set aside to drain.

2 Meanwhile, trim, wash and thinly slice the leeks. Peel and chop the onion and cut the courgettes into strips about the same size as the meat.

3 Heat the butter and 1 tbsp of the oil in a wok or large frying pan, add the turkey strips and stir-fry until the meat is just lightly browned. Remove from the pan and set aside.

4 Add the remaining oil to the pan, add the leeks and onion and stir-fry until just softened. Then add the courgette strips and continue to stir-fry until translucent.

5 Return the turkey to the pan and stir in the flour, then add the wine and stock and bring to the boil, stirring gently. Stir in the thyme and cream and season well.

6 Gently stir in the asparagus tips and pour into a shallow ovenproof dish. Mix together the breadcrumbs and Parmesan and sprinkle evenly over the top.

7 Bake in the oven for about 45 minutes until the topping is golden brown. Serve with crusty bread and a green salad.

Spiced Lamb Shanks

These melt-in-the mouth lamb shanks look stunning when coated with this rich, shimmering sauce.

preparation time
25 minutes

cooking time
2 hours

642 Kcal per portion

SERVES 4

- **Olive oil**, 1 tbsp
- **Butter**, 25g (1oz)
- **Lamb shanks**, 4
- **Small button or pickling onions**, 450g (1lb)
- **Oranges**, 2 large
- **Plain flour**, 2 tbsp
- **Mixed ground spice**, 2 tsp
- **Lamb or chicken stock**, 300ml (½ pint)
- **Prunes**, ready-to-eat, 250g (9oz)
- **Salt and freshly ground black pepper**

VARIATION

A tasty addition is 50g (2oz) of pine nut kernels. While the lamb is cooking, lightly toast the kernels under a grill (keep an eye on them because they will suddenly go brown) and set aside. When serving the lamb, sprinkle over the kernels.

1 Preheat the oven to 180°C/350°F/Gas 4. In a large flameproof casserole heat the olive oil and butter until sizzling, then add the lamb shanks and cook until browned, taking care not to let the oil and butter burn. Remove from the casserole and set aside.

2 Meanwhile, peel the onions, thinly pare the zest from the oranges (taking care not to remove too much of the white pith, as it will impart a bitter taste) and squeeze out the juice.

3 Add the onions to the casserole and cook for 2–3 minutes until lightly browned. Stir in the flour and spice and then add the orange zest and juice and stock.

4 Bring to the boil, stirring constantly, and then return the lamb shanks to the casserole and coat them well with the liquid.

5 Add the prunes and season well. Cover the surface closely with greaseproof paper to prevent excess evaporation, then cover with a lid and cook for 2 hours, turning over the lamb shanks after 1 hour.

6 Serve the lamb shanks on a bed of saffron rice or couscous.

Lancashire Hot Pot

For a special occasion you can add oysters to the hot pot, as was traditional in the days when they were plentiful and cheap.

 preparation time
30 minutes

 cooking time
2½ hours

505 Kcal per portion

SERVES 4

- **Olive oil,** 2–3 tbsp
- **Onions,** 2 large, peeled and thinly sliced
- **Carrots,** 500g (1lb 2oz), peeled and thinly sliced
- **Plain flour,** 3 tbsp
- **Salt and freshly ground black pepper**
- **Best end neck of lamb cutlets,** 8–12 lean, fat trimmed
- **Lamb or chicken stock,** 600ml (1 pint)
- **Large potatoes,** 900g (2lb), peeled and thinly sliced
- **Thyme sprigs,** 4–5
- **Butter,** 25g (1oz)

1 Preheat the oven to 180°C/350°F/Gas 4. Heat 1 tbsp of the oil in a large flameproof casserole.

2 Add the onions and cook for 2–3 minutes, until slightly softened. Remove from the casserole and set aside. Add the carrot to the casserole and cook for 1–2 minutes, then remove and mix with the onions.

3 Meanwhile, put the flour on a plate and season well. Dip the lamb cutlets in the flour until lightly coated on both sides, shaking off excess.

4 Heat the remaining oil in the casserole, add the cutlets and brown lightly on both sides, then remove from the casserole. Meanwhile, bring the stock to the boil in a saucepan.

5 Place half of the onion and carrots in the bottom of the casserole and then place the lamb cutlets on top of the vegetables. Add 2–3 sprigs of thyme, then cover with the remaining onion and carrots and season well.

6 Cover with closely packed and overlapping slices of potato. Pour the stock over the potatoes and dot with butter. Then season once more and place a sprig of thyme on top.

7 Cover the casserole with a lid or foil and cook in the oven for 1½ hours. Then uncover and continue cooking for 45–60 minutes until the potatoes are golden. Serve with pickled or cooked red cabbage.

COOK'S TIP
During cooking the top sprig of thyme becomes rather dried out. So just before serving, replace it with a fresh sprig, if wished.

Curried Lamb

A simple curry from the most traditional of ingredients.

 preparation time
25 minutes

 cooking time
2 hours

701 Kcal per portion

SERVES 4

- **Onions**, 2 large
- **Garlic cloves**, 2
- **Olive oil**, 2 tbsp
- **Boneless leg of lamb,** 1kg (2lb 4oz)
- **Medium hot curry powder**, 2 tbsp
- **Marsala curry paste,** 2 tbsp
- **Lamb or chicken stock,** 150ml (¼ pint)
- **Coconut milk**, 400ml can
- **Salt**
- **Coriander leaves**, a handful, to garnish

COOK'S TIPS

Ready-boned leg of lamb can be bought in most supermarkets.

Accompany the curry with raita and mango chutney.

VARIATIONS

If you prefer a really hot curry, use a hot curry powder.

Chicken or beef can also be used for making this curry.

1 Preheat the oven to 180°C/350°F/Gas 4. Peel and cut the onions in half lengthways, then cut the halves into thick slices lengthways. Peel and crush the garlic cloves.

2 Heat the oil in a large flameproof casserole, add the onions and garlic and cook until slighly softened and lightly browned. Remove from the casserole and set aside.

3 Meanwhile, remove skin and excess fat from the lamb and cut the flesh into 5cm (2in) pieces.

4 Add the lamb to the casserole and cook over a high heat until lightly browned (in two batches if necessary).

5 Stir the curry powder and paste into the meat and cook for just a few seconds, then return the onions to the casserole and add the stock and coconut milk. Mix together, season with salt and bring to the boil.

6 Cover the surface closely with greaseproof paper, then cover with a lid and cook in the oven for about 2 hours until the meat is tender. Serve sprinkled with coriander leaves and with warm naan bread or rice, or both.

Potato Bake

This dish can also be made with leftover cooked chicken or turkey.

**preparation time
20 minutes**

**cooking time
1¼ hours**

740 Kcal per portion

SERVES 6

- **Potatoes**, 1.3kg (3lb), peeled and thinly sliced
- **Salt and freshly ground black pepper**
- **Onion**, 1 large, peeled and thinly sliced
- **Frozen peas**, 150g (5oz)
- **Ham, thick slice**, 350g (12oz), fat removed and cubed
- **Gruyère cheese**, 150g (5oz), grated
- **Mixed dried herbs**, 1–2 tsp (optional)
- **Butter**, 25g (1oz)
- **Milk**, 300ml (½ pint)
- **Single cream**, 300ml (½ pint)

1 Preheat the oven to 220°C/425°F/Gas 7. Lightly butter a 25cm (10in) diameter shallow baking dish.

2 Arrange one-third of the potatoes in the bottom of the baking dish, overlapping them slightly. Season well and then arrange half of the sliced onions on top and scatter with half of the peas, half of the ham, one-third of the Gruyère cheese and half of the herbs.

3 Repeat step 2, then cover with the remaining potato slices, dot with butter and add the remaining cheese.

4 Whisk together the milk and cream, season well and carefully pour over the potatoes. Bake in the oven for 20 minutes.

5 Reduce the oven temperature to 180°C/350°F/Gas 4 and continue cooking for another 40–55 minutes, or until the top is golden brown and the potatoes are cooked. If necessary, loosely cover the dish with foil or greaseproof paper to prevent the potatoes from over-browning.

6 Remove from the oven and serve accompanied with a green salad and crusty bread.

COOK'S TIP

To make it safer to slice the potatoes, cut a thin sliver from the underside of each one. Alternatively, if you have one, use a mandolin cutter as this helps to speed up the preparation of the potatoes.

Spicy Pork & Bean Bake

Spanish chorizo gives this casserole a lovely hot and spicy Mediterranean flavour.

 preparation time
25 minutes

 cooking time
2 hours

614 Kcal per portion

SERVES 4

- **Pork loin steaks,** 4
- **Salt and freshly ground black pepper**
- **Butter,** 25g (1oz)
- **Olive oil,** 1 tbsp
- **Onions,** 2
- **Garlic clove,** 1 large
- **Chorizo sausage,** 110g (4oz) pack or piece
- **Cannellini beans,** 400g can
- **Dried oregano,** 2–3 tsp
- **Sugar,** 1 tsp
- **Tomatoes,** 400g can
- **Flat leaf parsley,** handful, for serving

1 Preheat the oven to 180°C/350°F/Gas 4. Pat the pork loin steaks dry with kitchen paper and season well.

2 In a large, shallow, flameproof casserole gently heat the butter and oil until sizzling and then add the steaks and cook for 2–3 minutes on each side until golden brown, taking care not to let the butter burn. Remove from the casserole and set aside.

3 Meanwhile, peel and slice the onions and garlic, slice the chorizo diagonally and rinse the beans. Add the onions and garlic to the casserole and cook for 3 minutes until softened.

4 Stir the oregano, sugar, beans and tomatoes into the onions and bring to the boil, then remove from the heat and return the pork steaks to the casserole and add the chorizo, coating all the meat well with the sauce.

5 Cover the surface closely with a sheet of greaseproof paper to prevent excess evaporation, and then cover the casserole with a lid or foil. Cook in the oven for 1½–2 hours until the pork is tender.

6 To serve, scatter parsley leaves over the top of each plateful and accompany with warmed rustic or French bread and a tossed green salad.

COOK'S TIP
Chorizo sausage can be bought pre-packed in linked or whole pieces, or from the delicatessen counter in most supermarkets.

VARIATION
This casserole can be made with loin steaks (as in this recipe) or loin chops or leg steaks.

West Country Sausage & Cider Casserole

West country ingredients – apples, cider and cream – combine to give this casserole a rich and delicious flavour.

 preparation time
25 minutes

 cooking time
2 hours

690 Kcal per portion

SERVES 6

- **Large potatoes,** 1.3kg (3lb), peeled and cut into 2.5cm (1in) cubes
- **Butter,** 75g (3oz)
- **Olive oil,** 1 tbsp
- **Thick pork sausages,** 12
- **Onions,** 2, peeled and chopped
- **Dessert apples,** 4, cored and cut in wedges
- **Plain flour,** 2 tbsp
- **Chicken or vegetable stock,** 250ml (8fl oz)
- **Strong cider,** 250ml (8fl oz)
- **Single cream,** 125ml (4fl oz)
- **Salt and freshly ground black pepper**
- **Sage leaves,** large handful

1 Preheat the oven to 180°C/350°F/Gas 4. Put the potatoes into a saucepan and cover them with water. Bring the water to the boil and then drain the potatoes and set aside.

2 Meanwhile, heat 25g (1oz) of the butter and the oil in a large casserole. Add the sausages and brown them lightly all over. Remove from the casserole and set aside.

3 Add the onions and the apple wedges and cook until the onions are softened. Stir in the flour and then add the stock and cider and bring to the boil, stirring constantly.

4 Remove the casserole from the heat and stir in the cream, season to taste and then add the sage leaves.

5 Return the sausages to the casserole, mix with the apples and onions and cover evenly with the drained potatoes.

6 Melt the remaining butter and drizzle it over the potatoes, then cook in the oven for 2 hours until the potato topping is golden brown and the potatoes are cooked. To prevent over-browning, cover the casserole with a lid or foil for the last 30 minutes.

7 Serve while piping hot, accompanied with broccoli or spring greens.

COOK'S TIPS

For the very best flavour, buy good quality pork sausages – preferably free-range – and a good strong cider.

If your casserole is shallow and wide rather than deep and narrow, you may need a few extra potatoes for the top.

Sweet 'n' Sour Pork

East meets West – the succulent sweet and sour sauce gives a subtle twist to a traditional pork casserole.

 preparation time
25 minutes

 cooking time
2 hours

541 Kcal per portion

SERVES 4

- **Boneless leg of pork,** 1.125kg (2½lb)
- **Olive oil,** 2 tbsp
- **Onion,** 1 large, peeled and chopped
- **Green pepper,** 1, cored, deseeded and sliced
- **Red pepper,** 1, cored, deseeded and sliced
- **Leeks,** 450g (1lb)
- **Garlic clove,** 1 large, peeled and crushed
- **Fresh ginger,** 25g (1oz), peeled and grated
- **Orange,** 1 small
- **Cornflour,** 2 tbsp
- **Soy sauce,** 2 tbsp
- **Rice vinegar,** 3 tbsp
- **Tomato purée,** 2 tbsp
- **Demerara sugar,** 2 tbsp
- **Chicken or vegetable stock,** 500ml (16fl oz)
- **Spring onions,** 4, trimmed and cut into ribbons

1 Preheat the oven to 180°C/350°F/ Gas 4. Remove the skin and excess fat from the pork and cut the flesh into 5cm (2in) pieces.

2 Heat the oil in a large casserole, add the pieces of pork (half at a time) and brown them lightly all over. Remove from the casserole and set aside.

3 Add the onion and peppers to the casserole and cook for 3–4 minutes, until slightly softened.

4 Meanwhile, wash and trim the leeks and cut in half widthways. Cut each piece in half lengthways and then cut lengthways into thin strips. Add to the casserole with the garlic and ginger and cook for 2–3 minutes.

5 Thinly pare the zest from the orange and add to the casserole. Squeeze and strain the juice from the orange into a measuring jug and then add the cornflour, soy sauce, vinegar, tomato purée and sugar. Stir well and make up to 600ml (1 pint) with stock.

6 Return the pork to the cassserole and add the stock. Mix gently and bring to the boil, then cover the surface with greaseproof paper to prevent excess evaporation. Cover the casserole with a lid and cook in the oven for 2 hours, until the pork is tender.

7 Sprinkle the spring onions over the casserole and serve accompanied with rice or noodles.

Oven-cooked Chilli

Cooking a chilli in the oven means that there is less risk of it catching and browning on the bottom.

preparation time
20 minutes

cooking time
1¼ hours

725 Kcal per portion

SERVES 4

- **Olive oil**, 1 tbsp
- **Butter**, 25g (1oz)
- **Onions**, 2 large, peeled and chopped
- **Garlic cloves**, 3, peeled and crushed
- **Lean, quality minced beef**, 1kg (2lb 4oz)
- **Hot chilli powder**, 1 tsp
- **Ground cumin**, 2 tsp
- **Tomatoes**, 2 x 400g cans
- **Sugar**, 1 tsp
- **Beef stock**, 250ml (8fl oz)
- **Red kidney beans**, 2 x 410g cans
- **Salt**
- **Fresh soured cream**, 150ml (¼ pint), to serve
- **Flat leaf parsley leaves**, a handful, to garnish

VARIATION

For a vegetarian version, omit the meat and replace with a chopped carrot and 400g can of cannellini beans. Alternatively, replace the beef mince with soya mince.

1 Preheat the oven to 180°C/350°F/Gas 4. Heat the oil and butter in a large flameproof casserole, add the onion and garlic and cook until slightly softened.

2 Add the beef to the casserole and cook over a high heat, stirring, until it changes colour. Then stir in the chilli powder and ground cumin and cook for 1–2 minutes.

3 Stir the tomatoes, sugar and stock into the meat, gently breaking up the tomatoes as you do so, then bring the contents of the casserole to the boil.

4 Meanwhile, pour the kidney beans into a colander, rinse then under a cold tap and drain them well. Stir the beans into the chilli and season with salt. Cover the casserole with a lid and cook in the oven for 1¼ hours.

5 Serve topped with spoonfuls of soured cream sprinkled with parsley. Serve with corn chips, soft flour tortillas or rice. Grated Cheddar cheese and diced avocado mixed with diced fresh tomatoes are the perfect accompaniments.

Speedy Lasagne

Normally, making a lasagne can seem to take up the best part of a day but this one can be put together in under 30 minutes.

 preparation time
25 minutes

 cooking time
45 minutes

778 Kcal per portion

SERVES 4

- **Olive oil**, 1 tbsp
- **Extra lean, quality minced beef**, 500g (1lb 2oz)
- **Bolognese sauce**, 500g bottle
- **Fresh Napoletana tomato sauce**, 350g tub
- **Butter**, 25g (1oz)
- **Plain flour**, 3 tbsp
- **Milk**, 600ml (1 pint)
- **Salt and freshly ground black pepper**
- **Nutmeg**
- **Fresh, ready-to-use lasagne**, 250g pack (approximately 13 sheets)
- **Parmesan cheese**, 50g (2oz), grated
- **Mozzarella cheese**, 125g pack, grated
- **Oregano**, dried, 2 tsp

1 Preheat the oven to 200°C/400°F/Gas 6. Heat the olive oil in a large frying pan, add the beef and stir over a high heat until it changes colour. Remove the pan from the heat and stir in the Bolognese and tomato sauces.

2 Melt the butter in a saucepan and stir in the flour, then add the milk and bring to the boil, stirring with a wire whisk until the sauce is thickened. Remove the pan from the heat and season sauce well with salt, pepper and freshly grated nutmeg.

3 Lightly oil a 30 x 20cm (12 x 8in) baking dish and place 4 sheets of lasagne in the bottom, cutting one in half lengthways to fit along the side of the first 3 sheets.

4 Spoon half of the beef sauce over the lasagne, then drizzle with a little of the white sauce and sprinkle with some of the Parmesan cheese. Add half the Mozzarella cheese and the oregano.

5 Add 4 more sheets of lasagne to the dish, repeat step 4 and then cover with the remaining sheets of lasagne, cutting to fit where necessary. Top with the remaining white sauce and Parmesan.

6 Place the dish on a baking tray and cook in the oven for 45 minutes, until the lasagne is golden brown. Remove from the oven and serve with a fresh green salad.

COOK'S TIP
You may think that the white sauce looks thinner than normal, but the ready-to-use lasagne sheets will absorb the liquid.

Hungarian Meatballs with Butterbeans

Sweet paprika and red and green peppers give this dish a typical Hungarian goulash flavour.

 preparation time
20 minutes

 cooking time
1 hour

500 Kcal per portion

SERVES 4

- **Extra lean, quality minced beef,** 500g (1lb 2oz)
- **Onions,** 1 small, 1 large, separately peeled and finely chopped
- **Mixed dried herbs,** 2 tsp
- **Sweet paprika,** 2 tsp
- **Fresh white breadcrumbs,** 6 tbsp
- **Olive oil,** 3 tbsp
- **Salt and freshly ground black pepper**
- **Butter,** 25g (1oz)
- **Green pepper,** 1 large, cored, deseeded and chopped
- **Red pepper,** 1 large, cored, deseeded and chopped
- **Garlic cloves,** 2, peeled and crushed
- **Chopped tomatoes,** 400g can
- **Sugar,** 1 tsp
- **Butterbeans,** 400g can
- **Basil,** large bunch

1 Preheat the oven to 180°C/350°F/Gas 4. Place the beef in a large mixing bowl and add the small chopped onion along with the herbs, paprika, breadcrumbs and 1 tbsp of the oil.

2 Season well and mix thoroughly together. Divide the mixture into 12 equal-sized pieces and shape into balls.

3 Heat the butter and 1 tbsp of the oil in a large flameproof casserole, add the meatballs and fry until lightly browned all over, taking care not to break them up as you turn them over. Remove from the casserole and set aside.

4 Heat the remaining oil in the casserole, add peppers and the remaining onion and cook gently until slightly softened. Mix in the garlic, tomatoes, sugar and butterbeans and season.

5 Carefully place the meatballs in the sauce, spooning it over as you do so. Bring to the boil, then cover with a tight-fitting lid and cook in the oven for 1 hour. Just before serving, finely shred and stir in the basil. Crusty bread and a green salad make good accompaniments to this dish.

Braised Steak with Guinness

After 2 hours of oven baking, the steak is thoroughly imbued with the flavour of Guinness.

preparation time
30 minutes

cooking time
2 hours

636 Kcal per portion

SERVES 4

- **Olive oil**, 2 tbsp
- **Onions**, 450g (1lb), peeled and sliced
- **Carrots**, 350g (12oz), peeled and sliced
- **Plain flour**, 3 tbsp
- **Salt and freshly ground black pepper**
- **Braising steak**, 1kg (2lb 4oz)
- **Butter**, 25g (1oz)
- **Fresh beef stock**, 300ml (½ pint)
- **Mixed dried herbs**, 1 tbsp
- **Guinness**, 500ml bottle
- **Button mushrooms**, 250g (9oz)
- **Parsley**, finely chopped, 2–3 tbsp, to garnish

COOK'S TIP

If the flavour of Guinness is too strong for you, a pale ale can be used instead.

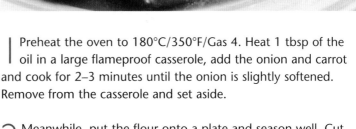

1 Preheat the oven to 180°C/350°F/Gas 4. Heat 1 tbsp of the oil in a large flameproof casserole, add the onion and carrot and cook for 2–3 minutes until the onion is slightly softened. Remove from the casserole and set aside.

2 Meanwhile, put the flour onto a plate and season well. Cut the beef into 10cm (4in) pieces, then dip in the flour and shake off excess. Heat the remaining oil and butter in the casserole, add the steak and brown lightly on both sides. Remove from the casserole and set aside.

3 Add the stock and bring to the boil, scraping the residue from the bottom of the pan. Reduce the heat and allow to boil gently for about 5 minutes until the stock is reduced by half.

4 Return the onions and carrots to the casserole, stir in the herbs and Guinness and bring to the boil. Then remove the casserole dish from the heat.

5 Add the mushrooms and steak and mix in gently, ensuring the meat is well covered with liquid. Cover the surface with greaseproof paper to prevent excess evaporation of the juices, then cover with a lid and cook in the oven for 2 hours.

6 Before serving, skim off any excess fat from the surface and sprinkle with parsley.

Side Dishes & Salads

These delicious and unusual vegetable accompaniments go
beautifully with the Weekday Dinners and Food for
Friends recipes given elsewhere in this book – or serve
them with your own favourite recipes. Find out how to
make the perfect mashed potato (p 127), discover new
twists on old standbys like peas and carrots, enjoy crisp,
delicious salads, or try a side dish like Cauliflower &
Broccoli Gratin (p 132) as a vegetarian main course.

Classic Potato Rosti

A classic potato dish from Switzerland, where it is often served at breakfast time with a fried or poached egg on top.

 preparation time
10 minutes

 cooking time
20 minutes

258 Kcal per portion
Suitable for vegetarians

SERVES 4

- **Waxy potatoes, such as Charlotte**, 675g (1½lb), about the size of eggs
- **Salt and freshly ground black pepper**
- **Butter**, 75g (3oz)
- **Parsley**, chopped, 2 tbsp

COOK'S TIP

If preferred, press all the potato into the frying pan to form one large round, and then cook as above. To turn it halfway through cooking, slide the rosti on to a plate. Serve cut into wedges.

1 Scrub the potatoes and place in a large saucepan. Cover with water and bring to the boil. Cook for 7 minutes and then drain well. Rinse under cold running water to cool.

2 Peel off the skins and coarsely grate the potato flesh into a bowl. Season and mix well, and then squeeze the mixture gently until it begins to hold together.

3 Melt the butter in a large frying pan over a low heat. Divide the mixture into 4 portions and form each into a round. Press each potato 'cake' into the pan using a palette knife to a thickness of about 2cm (¾in).

4 Fry gently for 5–7 minutes until the bottom is golden brown. Keep the heat low otherwise the butter may burn.

5 Turn over the rostis and cook for a further 5–7 minutes until golden and cooked through. Drain and serve sprinkled with chopped parsley.

Perfect Mashed Potato

The secret of a successful fluffy mash is plenty of butter and cream (or milk).
For something a bit more unusual, add Stilton or beetroot, as suggested here.

 preparation time
10 minutes

 cooking time
15 minutes

352 Kcal per portion
Suitable for vegetarians

SERVES 4

- **Floury potatoes,** 900g (2lb), peeled and thickly sliced
- **Salt**
- **Butter,** 110g (4oz)
- **Single cream,** 4 tbsp

1 Place the potatoes in a large saucepan with a large pinch of salt. Cover with water and bring to the boil. Cook for 10–12 minutes until tender to the point of a knife then drain well and return to the pan.

2 Add the butter and cream and mash well using a potato masher or large fork. Adjust the seasoning, if necessary, and serve.

VARIATIONS

LEEK AND STILTON MASH: melt 110g (4oz) butter in a frying pan and gently fry a large finely shredded leek for 4–5 minutes until softened but not browned. Add to the drained potato and mash well. Gently stir in 110g (4oz) crumbled mature Stilton cheese and adjust seasoning before serving.

BEETROOT MASH: add a 142ml carton soured cream to the drained potatoes and mash well, adjusting the seasoning to taste. Grate 110g (4oz) cooked beetroot in natural juice and serve the mash topped with the beetroot and sprinkled with a handful of caraway seeds.

Roasted Spring Vegetables

Baby and spring vegetables have a delicate flavour and for this reason they are usually steamed. However, roasting brings out their natural sweetness, while the herb butter adds a fresh taste.

 preparation time
5 minutes

 cooking time
25 minutes

238 Kcal per portion
Suitable for vegetarians

SERVES 4

- **Asparagus spears,** 175g (6oz), woody ends trimmed
- **Baby carrots,** 175g (6oz), trimmed and halved lengthways
- **Baby courgettes,** 110g (4oz), trimmed and halved lengthways
- **Baby corn,** 110g (4oz), trimmed
- **Sugarsnap peas,** 110g (4oz), topped and tailed
- **Baby leeks,** 4, trimmed
- **Olive oil,** 2 tbsp
- **Bay leaves,** 3
- **Salt and freshly ground black pepper**
- **Butter,** 75g (3oz), softened
- **Parsley,** chopped, 1 tbsp
- **Chives,** chopped, 1 tbsp
- **Tarragon,** chopped, 1 tbsp
- **Parsley, chives and tarragon,** extra for garnish (optional)

1 Preheat the oven to 220°C/425°F/Gas 7. Wash and pat dry all the vegetables and place in a large bowl. Toss in the olive oil, bay leaves and plenty of seasoning.

2 Pile into a large, shallow-sided baking tray and spread out into an even layer. Bake in the oven for about 25 minutes, turning occasionally, until tender and lightly golden.

3 Meanwhile, place the butter in a bowl and mix in the chopped herbs and some seasoning. Mix well, cover and chill until ready to serve so the butter is firm enough to slice well.

4 To serve, discard the bay leaves, drain the vegetables well and place in a serving dish. Top with dots of herb butter and garnish with fresh herbs, if liked.

COOK'S TIP
If time is short, you can chill the butter in super-quick time by placing it in the freezer for 10 minutes or so.

Peas with Lettuce & Mint

Peas are a real family favourite, but in this dish they are given a sophisticated twist thanks to the fresh summery flavours of lettuce and mint.

 preparation time
5 minutes

 cooking time
20 minutes

149 Kcal per portion
Suitable for vegetarians

SERVES 4

- **Butter,** 25g (1oz)
- **Onion,** 1, peeled and finely chopped
- **Fresh peas in pods,** 675g (1½lb) or frozen peas, 400g (14oz)
- **Sugarsnap peas,** 175g (6oz)
- **Caster sugar,** 1 tsp
- **Mint sprigs,** 4
- **Little Gem lettuce,** 2
- **Salt**
- **Crushed black pepper**

VARIATIONS

For a contrast of flavour, replace the Little Gem lettuce with a bitter leaf such as chicory or use shredded radicchio for added colour and flavour, using basil instead of mint.

1 Melt the butter in a small frying pan, add the onion and gently fry over a low heat for 10 minutes until just softened but not browned. Then set aside.

2 Meanwhile, shell the peas if using fresh, and top, tail and cut the sugarsnap peas in half diagonally. Bring a saucepan of lightly salted water to the boil and cook the fresh peas with the sugar and some of the mint (reserving the rest for garnishing) for 8–10 minutes if young, or 10–15 minutes if older. If using frozen peas, cook according to the manufacturer's instructions.

3 Cook the sugarsnap peas with the other peas for 5 minutes. Drain well, return to the saucepan and discard the mint.

4 While the peas are cooking, wash and shake dry the lettuce, and then shred finely. Set aside.

5 To serve, toss the shredded lettuce and cooked onion along with the cooking juices into the drained peas. Add salt to taste. Pile into a warmed serving dish and serve sprinkled with crushed black pepper and the remaining fresh mint.

Spiced Steamed Carrots

This is a lovely, light and zingy vegetable dish, perfect to serve with chicken or fish.

preparation time
10 minutes

cooking time
10 minutes

92 Kcal per portion
Suitable for vegetarians

SERVES 4

- **Carrots,** 7, peeled and cut into thin batons
- **Root ginger,** 2.5cm (1in) piece, peeled and grated
- **Spring onions,** 6, trimmed and finely chopped
- **Low-fat natural yogurt,** 150g (5oz)
- **Lemon zest,** finely grated, ½ tsp
- **Lemon juice,** freshly squeezed, 1 tbsp
- **Clear honey,** 1 tsp
- **Light soy sauce,** 1 tbsp

1 Place the carrots in a large bowl. Then add the ginger and all but 2 tbsp of the spring onions and mix well.

2 Bring a large saucepan of lightly salted water to the boil. Place the carrot mixture in a steaming compartment or large colander or sieve and sit on top of the water. Cover and steam for 10 minutes, turning occasionally, until tender.

3 Meanwhile, place the yogurt in a small bowl. Add the lemon zest and juice, honey and soy sauce and mix together. Cover the dressing until it is required.

4 To serve, pile the carrots into a warmed serving dish and drizzle with the lemon yogurt. Serve immediately, sprinkled with the reserved chopped spring onions, if liked.

COOK'S TIP

Use ready-prepared grated or minced fresh ginger for convenience. Available in jars, it is usually sold in the herb and spice section of the supermarket or grocer. Store in the fridge after opening.

Cauliflower & Broccoli Gratin

Based on the traditional favourite cauliflower cheese, this recipe combines florets of cauliflower and broccoli with a tasty cheese sauce.

 preparation time
12 minutes

 cooking time
12 minutes

498 Kcal per portion
Suitable for vegetarians

SERVES 4

- **Cauliflower**, 450g (1lb)
- **Broccoli**, 450g (1lb)
- **Milk**, 600ml (1 pint)
- **Cornflour**, 2 tbsp
- **Mature Cheddar cheese**, 225g (8oz), grated
- **Salt and freshly ground black pepper**
- **Fresh white breadcrumbs**, 4 tbsp
- **Chopped mixed nuts**, 2 tbsp
- **Tomatoes**, 4

1 Remove the stalk from the cauliflower and break into even-sized florets about 5cm (2in) in length.

2 Discard about 5cm (2in) of the broccoli stalk and then cut into florets the same size as the cauliflower.

3 Bring a large saucepan of lightly salted water to the boil, add the florets and cook for 6–7 minutes until just tender. Drain very well, so that the sauce is not watery, and place in an ovenproof gratin dish; cover and keep warm.

4 Meanwhile, in a cup blend a little of the milk with the cornflour to form a paste. Transfer to a saucepan and then stir in the rest of the milk.

5 Heat gently, stirring, until boiling and the sauce thickens. Remove from the heat and stir in all but 50g (2oz) of the cheese and season to taste.

6 Preheat the grill to a medium/hot setting. Spoon the sauce over the vegetables and sprinkle evenly with the remaining cheese and the breadcrumbs and chopped nuts. Cook under the grill for 4–5 minutes until melted, bubbling and lightly golden.

7 To serve, deseed and chop the tomatoes finely and serve the gratin with some chopped tomatoes spooned on top.

COOK'S TIP
This recipe is ideal served as an accompaniment to grilled sausages or roast gammon or as a vegetarian main course with baked potatoes.

VARIATION
For a tangy taste, try Cotswold cheese with chives in place of the Cheddar.

Stir-fried Brussels Sprouts with Cabbage & Orange

A new take on two old favourites, this dish is a delicious accompaniment to a roast dinner.

**preparation time
10 minutes**

**cooking time
10 minutes**

212 Kcal per portion

SERVES 4

- **Brussels sprouts**, 350g (12oz)
- **Savoy cabbage**, 350g (12oz)
- **Butter**, 25g (1oz)
- **Vegetable oil**, 1 tbsp
- **Rindless streaky bacon rashers**, 4, chopped
- **Onion**, 1, peeled and finely sliced
- **Worcestershire sauce**, 2 tbsp
- **Orange juice**, freshly squeezed, 2 tbsp
- **Orange zest**, finely grated, ½ tsp
- **Clear honey**, 2 tsp
- **Salt and freshly ground black pepper**

1 Trim the Brussels sprouts and shred them finely. Discard any outer damaged leaves from the cabbage, slice out the central core and then shred the leaves very finely.

2 Melt the butter with the oil in a wok or large frying pan and stir-fry the bacon and onion for 4–5 minutes until just softened. Add the Brussels sprouts, cabbage and Worcestershire sauce and stir-fry over a high heat for 4–5 minutes until just tender.

3 Remove the wok or pan from the heat and stir in the orange juice and zest and the honey, and season well. Serve immediately.

COOK'S TIP
This dish makes the perfect accompaniment to a Christmas roast turkey. To make it easier to prepare in the Christmas rush, stir-fry the onion and bacon and chop the cabbage and sprouts the day before, ready for last minute stir-frying and dressing.

VARIATION
If preferred, you can use other cabbages such as red or white in place of the Savoy cabbage.

Tempura Vegetables with Chilli Dip

This batter cooks to a golden crisp and provides the perfect casing for vegetables. It is also good with shellfish.

preparation time
15 minutes

cooking time
15 minutes

395 Kcal per portion
Suitable for vegetarians

SERVES 4

- **Plain flour,** 75g (3oz)
- **Milk,** 150ml (¼ pint)
- **Egg,** 1
- **Dark soy sauce,** 3 tbsp
- **Corn oil,** 2 litres (3½ pints)
- **Sweet chilli sauce,** 6 tbsp
- **Dry sherry,** 3 tbsp
- **Red pepper,** 1
- **Yellow pepper,** 1
- **Carrot,** 1 large
- **Baby corn,** 110g (4oz)
- **Spring onions,** 1 bunch
- **Baby courgettes,** 110g (4oz)
- **Cornflour,** 2 tbsp
- **Cream of tartar,** ½ tsp
- **Chinese leaves,** to serve

VARIATIONS

Other vegetables to try are thin asparagus spears, open cup mushrooms, mangetout, strips of larger courgette, orange sweet potatoes, peeled and sliced, and aubergine slices.

1 For the batter, sift the flour into a small bowl. Gradually mix in the milk along with the egg, 1 tbsp soy sauce and 1 tbsp corn oil. Set the batter aside.

2 For the dip, mix together the remaining soy sauce, the sweet chilli sauce and dry sherry. Set aside until ready to serve.

3 Core, halve and deseed the peppers and cut into thick slices. Peel the carrot and cut into long thin slices. Trim the baby corn. Trim away the tops and roots from the spring onions. Trim the courgettes and cut in half lengthways.

4 Place all the vegetables in a large bowl and toss them in the cornflour, until well dusted all over.

5 Pour the corn oil into a large saucepan and heat until 190°C/375°F. Whisk the cream of tartar into the batter mixture. Pour the batter over the vegetables and mix well to coat.

6 Deep-fry the vegetables in 3 batches for 3–4 minutes until crisp and golden. Drain well and keep warm while cooking each batch. Serve the tempura vegetables on a bed of shredded Chinese leaves, with the chilli sauce.

Parched Corn with Chilli Butter

This recipe is perfect for a barbecue, but if it's rained off, the cobs will cook just as well under a hot grill.

preparation time
8 minutes

cooking time
7 minutes

226 Kcal per portion
Suitable for vegetarians

SERVES 6

- **Butter**, 75g (3oz), softened
- **Hot chilli powder**, ½ tsp
- **Paprika**, 1 tsp
- **Coriander, chopped**, 1 tbsp
- **Salt and freshly ground black pepper**
- **Sweetcorn cobs**, 4

1 Place the butter in a bowl and mix in the chilli powder, paprika, coriander and seasoning. Mix well, cover and chill until ready to serve.

2 Remove the leaves and husk from the sweetcorn. Bring a large saucepan of water to the boil and cook the sweetcorn, covered, for 2 minutes. Drain well, shaking off the excess water, and set aside until ready to grill.

3 Cook the cobs over medium coals for 4–5 minutes, turning frequently, until lightly charred. Serve with the flavoured butter to melt over.

COOK'S TIP

If you don't like your sweetcorn cobs charred, you may choose to retain some of the smaller, inner leaves, in which case tie clean string around the cob to ensure they stay in place. The leaves will act as protection from fierce heat. Alternatively, wrap the sweetcorn cobs – with or without their leaves – in foil, which will have the same effect.

Roast Vegetable Salad with Cucumber Raita

Full of Mediterranean flavours and colours, this salad makes a substantial side dish, or even a tasty main meal.

preparation time
10 minutes

cooking time
20 minutes

405 Kcal per portion
Suitable for vegetarians

SERVES 4

- **Red onion**, 1, peeled and sliced
- **Lemon juice**, 1 tbsp
- **Fennel bulb**, 1, trimmed and sliced
- **Red pepper**, 1, cored, deseeded and chopped
- **Yellow pepper**, 1, cored, deseeded and chopped
- **Green pepper**, 1, cored, deseeded and chopped
- **Garlic cloves**, 2, peeled and sliced
- **Salt and freshly ground black pepper**
- **Olive oil**, 4 tbsp
- **Couscous**, 250g (9oz)
- **Sweet chilli sauce**, 4 tbsp
- **Wholegrain mustard**, 2 tbsp
- **Cucumber**, ¼ whole
- **Low-fat natural yogurt**, 150g (5oz)

1 Preheat the oven to 220°C/425°F/Gas 7. Place the onion in a large bowl and toss in the lemon juice and sliced fennel.

2 Add the peppers and garlic cloves, plenty of seasoning and the olive oil and stir together thoroughly.

3 Pile the vegetables onto a large, shallow-sided baking tray and spread out evenly. Bake in the oven for 20 minutes, turning occasionally, until the vegetables are tender and lightly charred.

4 Meanwhile, prepare the couscous according to the manufacturer's instructions. Mix together the chilli sauce and mustard and set aside.

5 Finely chop the cucumber and mix into the natural yogurt. Season, cover and chill until required.

6 To serve, drain the vegetables and transfer to a heatproof serving bowl. Toss in the chilli and mustard mixture and carefully mix in the couscous. Serve with the raita.

VARIATIONS
You can serve this recipe hot or cold. For a main course, add warmed pitta breads and a crisp leaf salad with sweet cherry tomatoes. If preferred, replace the couscous with leftover cooked rice.

FREEZING
Suitable for freezing without the cucumber raita.

Sunshine Salad

A colourful combination of shredded vegetables, which will brighten up any meal or packed lunch.

**preparation time
20 minutes**

**235 Kcal per portion
Suitable for vegetarians**

SERVES 4

- **Celery stalks with leaves,** 6, stalks sliced and leaves shredded
- **Radishes,** 110g (4oz), coarsley grated
- **Carrots,** 3 large
- **Oranges,** 5
- **Walnut pieces,** 50g (2oz)
- **Low-fat natural fromage frais,** 4 tbsp
- **Walnut oil,** 1 tbsp
- **Clear honey,** 1 tsp
- **Salt and freshly ground black pepper**

VARIATIONS

When in season, celeriac root makes a wonderful addition to this salad. Replace 4 celery stalks with 450g (1lb) celeriac root. Trim and peel the knobbly skin from the celeriac and then either coarsely grate or shred finely. Toss in 2 tbsp orange juice to stop it from discolouring.

For a more substantial dish add cooked chicken or prawns.

1 Place the celery stalks and leaves in a large bowl. Add the radish and carrot, mix together and cover and chill.

2 Meanwhile, slice off the tops and bottoms from 4 of the oranges. Using a sharp knife, slice off the skin, removing the pith at the same time. Over a bowl, cut out the orange flesh by slicing along the side of the membranes dividing the segments, letting the juice and segments fall into the bowl.

3 Gently mix the segments and juice into the prepared celery mixture along with the walnut pieces, cover and chill.

4 For the dressing, finely grate ½ tsp orange zest from the remaining orange and extract 1 tbsp juice. Mix the zest and juice into the fromage frais together with the walnut oil, honey and plenty of seasoning.

5 To serve, pile the vegetable and orange salad into a large serving bowl and drizzle over the fromage frais dressing.

Tuna Caesar-style Salad

An ever-popular salad, but this time with the addition
of tuna flakes and sweet cherry tomatoes.

preparation time
25 minutes

296 Kcal per portion

SERVES 4

- **Butter**, 25g (1oz), softened
- **Garlic clove**, 1, peeled and crushed
- **Parsley**, chopped, 2 tsp
- **Salt and freshly ground black pepper**
- **French bread**, 4 thick slices cut on the diagonal
- **Crisp lettuce**, 1
- **Cherry tomatoes**, 110g (4oz)
- **Tuna in spring water**, 2 x 160g cans, drained
- **Anchovy fillets**, 50g can, drained
- **Pitted black olives in brine**, 50g (2oz), drained
- **Capers in brine**, 2 tbsp, drained
- **Caesar-style dressing**, 4 tbsp
- **Parmesan cheese**, 25g (1oz)

1 Mix the butter with the garlic and parsley. Season well and set aside. Preheat the grill to a hot setting and lightly toast the bread on both sides. Set aside.

2 Discard any damaged outer leaves from the lettuce. Break into pieces, discard the stem and tough stalks and rinse in cold water. Shake dry and place in a salad bowl. Wash and pat dry the tomatoes, then cut in half and add to the lettuce.

3 Flake the tuna into bite-sized pieces and roughly chop the anchovy fillets. Gently toss into the salad along with the olives, capers and dressing.

4 Just before serving, spread the toasted bread with the garlic butter on one side and put under the grill until the butter has melted and the bread is golden.

5 To serve, place a piece of garlic bread on each serving plate. Top with some salad. Using a vegetable peeler, pare off thin pieces of Parmesan and add to the salad. Serve immediately.

Food for Friends

No matter how much you enjoy cooking, there are

always times when you want to create a feast with

the minimum of fuss. This chapter has been

designed with just this in mind and here we give

you main meal dishes that will impress and taste

good – and yet only take 30 minutes to prepare

and cook. With these recipes, entertaining can be

as much fun for you as it is for your guests.

Baked Trout with Tabbouleh

This fresh, healthy stuffing — nutty bulghar wheat combined with chopped vegetables and some added lemon zing — goes well with the delicate flavour of trout.

**preparation time
15 minutes**

**cooking time
15 minutes**

346 Kcal per portion

SERVES 4

- **Bulghar wheat,** 75g (3oz)
- **Cucumber,** 2.5cm (1in)
- **Spring onions,** 2
- **Ripe tomato,** 1
- **Mint,** a small bunch
- **Lemon,** 2
- **Whole, cleaned trout,**
  4 x 225g (8oz)
- **Salt and freshly ground
  black pepper**
- **Bay leaves,** 4
- **Butter,** 25g (1oz)

1 Preheat the oven to 230°C/450°F/Gas 8. Place the bulghar wheat in a heatproof bowl and cover with boiling water. Stand for 10 minutes.

2 Meanwhile, finely chop the cucumber. Trim and finely chop the spring onions. Finely chop the tomato. Reserving a few sprigs of mint for garnish, roughly chop the remainder. Finely grate the zest and extract the juice from 1 lemon.

3 Wash and pat dry the trout and season inside. Drain the bulghar wheat well, and mix in the chopped vegetables, mint, lemon zest and plenty of seasoning. Pack this mixture into the centre of each trout.

4 Place the trout in a shallow baking dish lined with baking parchment and lay a bay leaf on each fish. Sprinkle over the lemon juice and top each trout with a knob of butter. Bake the fish in the oven for 15 minutes, until tender and cooked through.

5 Drain the trout and discard the bay leaves. Serve sprinkled with the remaining mint, roughly chopped, accompanied with warmed, lightly toasted pitta breads, some crisp salad leaves and wedges of fresh lemon to squeeze over.

VARIATION
In place of the bulghar wheat, use couscous or cooked rice.

Seafood with Rice Towers

Scallops and prawns give any meal a special-occasion feel while moulding the rice gives this dish a smart restaurant look.

**preparation time
10 minutes**

**cooking time
15 minutes**

290 Kcal per portion

SERVES 4

- **Basmati rice**, 150g (5oz), rinsed well
- **Tiger prawns**, raw, shell on, 12
- **Scallops**, 8
- **Butter**, 50g (2oz)
- **Garlic clove**, 1, crushed
- **Coriander**, chopped, 5 tbsp plus sprigs for garnishing
- **Mild chilli powder**, ½ tsp
- **Ground cinnamon**, good pinch
- **Lime**, 1, grated zest and juice
- **Salt and freshly ground pepper**

1 Put the rice in a saucepan, with enough cold water to cover by 12mm (½in). Put the lid on the pan, bring to the boil and then reduce the heat to its lowest setting and simmer for 8–10 minutes until just tender.

2 Meanwhile, shell the prawns and remove the tough muscle from the scallops and clean the corals if there are any. Rinse and dry the shellfish.

3 Drain the rice. Put a quarter of the butter and all the crushed garlic into the pan, let it sizzle and then stir in the rice and coriander. Lightly pack the rice into warmed dariole moulds and keep warm until the dish is served.

4 Heat a frying pan, add the rest of the butter, the chilli powder and cinnamon and then the prawns and scallops in one layer. Cook for 2 minutes. Turn over the shellfish and sprinkle with the zest and juice from half the lime to start with, adding more zest and juice and seasoning, to taste.

5 Turn each rice tower out onto a warmed dinner plate. Spoon the seafood and the buttery sauce around each one and garnish with a sprig of coriander. Serve with some sugarsnap peas mixed with chopped tomatoes or salad.

COOK'S TIPS

There's no need to grease the moulds for the rice as they slip out very easily, just like making sandcastles! If you don't have dariole moulds, use small tea cups instead.

Salmon Florentine

Salmon and spinach are a winning combination while the addition of rocket gives the dish a slightly peppery flavour.

**preparation time
10 minutes**

**cooking time
15 minutes**

421 Kcal per portion

SERVES 4

- **Salmon fillets,** 4 x 150g (5oz), skinned
- **Bay leaves,** 2
- **Dry white wine,** 150ml (¼ pint)
- **Fish stock,** 150ml (¼ pint)
- **Salt and freshly ground black pepper**
- **Baby spinach leaves,** 450g (1lb)
- **Wild rocket,** 50g (2oz)
- **Leeks,** 2 large
- **Crème fraîche or extra thick double cream,** 4 tbsp
- **Ground nutmeg,** ½ tsp

1 Wash and pat dry the salmon and place in a shallow frying pan with a lid. Add the bay leaves and pour in the wine and stock. Season and bring to the boil.

2 Cover and simmer for 6–7 minutes until just cooked through. Turn off the heat and allow to stand until required.

3 Meanwhile, rinse the spinach and rocket, and pack into a large saucepan while wet. Trim the leeks and split open lengthways. Rinse under cold running water to remove any trapped earth. Shake well to remove excess water, slice finely and then, reserving a little for garnish, mix into the wet spinach and rocket.

4 Cover the saucepan and place on a medium/high heat for about 8 minutes, turning halfway through, until wilted – the vegetables will cook in the steam. Put the reserved leeks into a steamer over the spinach and leek mixture. Don't have the heat too high otherwise the vegetables will burn on the bottom of the saucepan.

5 Drain the vegetables well by pressing against the side of a colander or sieve to remove as much water as possible.

6 Transfer the spinach mixture to a food processor and add the crème fraîche or cream, nutmeg and seasoning, and blend for a few seconds until smooth.

7 To serve, divide the spinach mixture between warmed serving plates. Drain the salmon and place on top of the spinach. Dust with more ground nutmeg and black pepper, if liked, and garnish with reserved leek. Serve with buttered new potatoes.

VARIATIONS

Replace the wine with all fish stock and, for a healthier version, replace the crème fraîche with low-fat natural fromage frais.

You can use all spinach in place of the spinach and rocket and for a coarser texture, chop the spinach and leek on a board rather than blending.

Salmon & Asparagus Pasta

This fresh-tasting and colourful pasta dish is as healthy as it is delicious.

 preparation time
5 minutes

 cooking time
15 minutes

566 Kcal per portion

SERVES 4

- **Tagliatelle**, 300g (11oz)
- **Salt and freshly ground black pepper**
- **Salmon fillets**, 600g (1lb 5oz)
- **Bay leaf**, 1
- **Fish stock**, 300ml (½ pint)
- **Fine asparagus**, 225g (8oz), woody ends trimmed, tips cut into short lengths
- **Fennel bulb**, 1, sliced
- **Low-fat natural fromage frais**, 225g (8oz)
- **Dill**, chopped, 2 tbsp

1 Bring a large saucepan of lightly salted water to the boil and cook the tagliatelle according to the manufacturer's instructions. Drain well and return to the pan.

2 Meanwhile, wash and pat dry the salmon fillets and place in a frying pan with a lid. Add the bay leaf and pour over the stock, bring to the boil, cover and simmer for 3 minutes.

3 Add the asparagus and fennel to the salmon and cook for another 3–4 minutes until the salmon is cooked through and the vegetables are tender.

4 Drain the salmon and vegetables. Carefully flake the salmon away from the skin. Gently toss the salmon flesh into the pasta along with the vegetables, fromage frais and chopped dill. Adjust seasoning and serve immediately.

COOK'S TIP
Serve with a crisp salad and lemon wedges to squeeze over the pasta.

VARIATION
In place of the tagliatelle, use wholemeal pasta, which gives extra 'bite' to the dish and has a slightly nuttier flavour.

Tricolore Chunky White Fish

Fish takes on a rustic Italian flavour when baked with tomatoes, olives and basil.

 **preparation time
5 minutes**

 **cooking time
25 minutes**

293 Kcal per portion

SERVES 4

- **Thick white fish fillets, such as cod,** 4 x 175g (6oz), skinned
- **Salt and freshly ground black pepper**
- **Chopped tomatoes with garlic,** 400g can
- **Mozzarella cheese,** 150g (5oz), thinly sliced
- **Marinated black olives in olive oil,** 75g (3oz)
- **Basil leaves,** a handful, to garnish

1 Preheat the oven to 220°C/425°F/Gas 7. Wash and pat dry the fish fillets and season on both sides. Place in a shallow baking dish.

2 Spoon the chopped tomatoes over the fish. Sprinkle evenly with the olives and their oil.

3 Bake in the oven for 20–25 minutes until tender and cooked through. After 10 minutes, arrange the slices of cheese on top. Serve sprinkled with basil leaves and black pepper.

COOK'S TIP
Accompany this simple fish dish with some warm, crusty Italian bread to mop up the tomato sauce, and either some freshly steamed vegetables such as asparagus tips and baby carrots or a crisp, colourful salad.

Crispy Crumb-crusted Chicken

Fried chicken flavour without all the calories of deep-fat frying.

 preparation time
5 minutes

 cooking time
25 minutes

344 Kcal per portion

SERVES 4

- **Mayonnaise**, 3 tbsp
- **Sun-dried tomato purée**, 1 tbsp
- **Fresh white breadcrumbs**, 4 tbsp
- **Parmesan cheese**, grated, 2 tbsp
- **Boneless chicken breasts**, 4, skinned
- **Freshly ground black pepper**
- **Olive oil**, 2 tbsp
- **Basil leaves**, a handful, to garnish

COOK'S TIP

It's easy to put together an Italian-style salad. Mix rocket, basil and radicchio leaves, lightly chopped plum tomato, and then simply drizzle with balsamic vinegar and a little olive oil.

1 Preheat the oven to 200°C/400°F/Gas 6. Mix together the mayonnaise and tomato purée, and then mix together the breadcrumbs and cheese. Set aside.

2 Wash and pat dry the chicken breasts with kitchen paper. Place on a baking sheet lined with baking parchment. Season with black pepper.

3 Spread the chicken breasts thickly with 1 tbsp of the tomato mayonnaise, and then pat on the breadcrumb mixture, pressing it on to make sure the chicken is well coated.

4 Drizzle each breast with olive oil and then bake in the oven for 20–25 minutes until golden, tender and cooked through. Serve hot accompanied with the remaining mayonnaise, a fresh mixed salad and a sprinkling of fresh basil.

Tarragon Chicken

Tarragon is the perfect complement to chicken.

preparation time
5 minutes

cooking time
25 minutes

358 Kcal per portion

SERVES 4

- **Boneless chicken breasts,** 4, skinned
- **Salt and freshly ground black pepper**
- **Olive oil,** 2 tbsp
- **Cornflour,** 1½ tbsp
- **Dry white wine,** 150ml (¼ pint)
- **Chicken stock,** 150ml (¼ pint)
- **Double cream,** 6 tbsp
- **Tarragon,** chopped, 3 tbsp

1 Wash and pat dry the chicken breasts and season on both sides. Heat the oil in a frying pan and cook the chicken for about 8 minutes on each side until golden and cooked through.

2 Remove the chicken from the pan with a slotted spoon and keep warm while you make the sauce.

3 In the same frying pan, blend the cornflour with the pan juices and gradually blend in the wine. Pour in the chicken stock and bring to the boil, stirring, until thickened. Simmer for 1 minute then add the cream.

4 Remove from the heat, season with black pepper and stir in the tarragon. Add the chicken to the sauce and heat through, spooning the sauce over the chicken, for about 2 minutes. Serve with steamed carrots and sautéed potatoes.

COOK'S TIP
Use a mild or weaker chicken stock for this recipe so as not to overpower the flavour of the tarragon.

Stuffed Chicken Breasts

Slices of Parma ham are a sophisticated finishing touch, perfect for a dinner party.

 preparation time
10 minutes

 cooking time
25 minutes

508 Kcal per portion

SERVES 4

- **Chicken breasts,** 5 small, skinned
- **Whipping cream,** 1 tbsp
- **Parmesan cheese,** grated, 1 tbsp
- **Hazelnuts,** toasted and chopped, 2–3 tbsp
- **Sun-dried tomatoes,** 50g (2oz), drained
- **Parma ham,** 8 slices
- **Salt and freshly ground black pepper**

FOR THE SAUCE

- **Flour,** 1 tsp
- **Whipping cream,** 200ml (7fl oz)
- **Nutmeg,** grated
- **Hazelnuts,** toasted and chopped, 1 tbsp

1 Preheat the oven to 180°C/350°F/Gas 5. Take one of the chicken breasts, chop it roughly and put into the food processor. Add the cream, Parmesan, hazelnuts and sun-dried tomatoes and blend. Season well.

2 Lay the remaining chicken breasts on the work surface and open them out, slicing them open if need be to make a wide flat surface.

3 Take the chicken mince and form into 4 sausage-like shapes. Lay these along each breast and wrap the meat around to enclose the filling. Wrap each chicken breast in 2 slices of Parma ham to enclose completely and arrange on a baking sheet. Bake in the oven for 25 minutes.

4 To make the sauce, whisk the flour into the cream in a saucepan and heat slowly, whisking constantly until thickened. Season with salt, pepper and nutmeg. Add the hazelnuts.

5 Slice the chicken rolls thickly and fan out the meat on warm plates. Pour a little sauce around and serve with lightly steamed runner beans.

COOK'S TIP

To toast hazelnuts, put them on a baking tray in a hot oven for about 5 minutes. Take them out and allow to cool a little before rubbing off the skins.

Coq au Vin

This classic French dish usually takes hours, but you can have it on the table in minutes.

 preparation time
5 minutes

 cooking time
25 minutes

415 Kcal per portion

SERVES 4

- **Plain flour,** 2 tbsp
- **Salt and freshly ground black pepper**
- **Boneless chicken thighs,** 8, skinned
- **Rindless streaky bacon rashers,** 4
- **Shallots,** 8
- **Butter,** 50g (2oz)
- **Dry red wine,** 300ml (½ pint)
- **Chicken stock,** 150ml (¼ pint)
- **Bouquet garni,** 1 fresh or dried
- **Caster sugar,** 2 tsp
- **Button mushrooms,** 225g (8oz), wiped
- **Dijon mustard,** 2 tsp
- **Parsley,** chopped, 2 tbsp

COOK'S TIP

Bouquet garni is a French term for a small bunch of herbs – bay leaf, thyme, rosemary, tarragon and parsley – tied together and added to soups, casseroles and stocks to impart flavour.

1 Sprinkle the flour on a plate and season well. Wash and pat dry the chicken thighs, and slice in half lengthways; then toss thoroughly in the flour. Roughly chop the bacon, and toss in the flour as well.

2 Peel the shallots and halve if large. Melt the butter in a large frying pan and gently fry the chicken, bacon and shallots with all the flour, turning occasionally, for about 10 minutes until browned all over.

3 Pour in the wine and stock, mixing well, until blended. Add the bouquet garni and sugar. Bring to the boil and simmer, uncovered, for 10 minutes.

4 Add the mushrooms and mustard and continue to cook for a further 5 minutes, stirring, until tender and cooked through. Discard the bouquet garni.

5 To serve, spoon on to warmed serving plates and sprinkle with chopped parsley and accompany with steamed broccoli florets and French bread to mop up the sauce.

Turkey & Pepper Kebabs

A cheerful recipe fit to adorn any supper table – the chunks of pineapple in the sauce add a tang to the sweetness of the multi-coloured peppers on the kebabs.

 preparation time
10 minutes

 cooking time
20 minutes

304 Kcal per portion

SERVES 4

- **Boneless turkey breasts,** 450g (1lb), skinned
- **Garlic clove,** 1
- **Butter,** 50g (2oz), melted
- **Red pepper,** 1
- **Yellow pepper,** 1
- **Green pepper,** 1
- **Onion,** 1
- **Spring onions,** 1 bunch
- **Pineapple pieces in natural juice,** 227g can
- **Chicken stock,** 150ml (¼ pint)
- **White wine vinegar,** 2 tbsp
- **Caster sugar,** 1 tbsp
- **Tomato purée,** 2 tbsp
- **Salt and freshly ground black pepper**

1 Cut the turkey into 2cm (¾in) thick chunks and place in a bowl. Peel and crush the garlic and toss into the turkey along with the melted butter, stirring well until thoroughly coated.

2 Core, halve and deseed the peppers, and cut into chunks. Peel the onion and slice into thick wedges.

3 Thread pieces of pepper, onion and turkey on to 8 skewers. Preheat the grill to a medium setting and cook the kebabs for 10 minutes on each side, until golden and cooked through.

4 Meanwhile, make the sauce. Trim and chop the spring onions and place in a saucepan along with the pineapple pieces and the canning juice.

5 Add the stock, vinegar, sugar, tomato purée and seasoning. Bring to the boil, stirring, and then simmer for 2 minutes.

6 To serve, drain the kebabs well and serve on a bed of rice accompanied with the hot sauce.

COOK'S TIP

You will need to use the canning juice from the pineapple for making the sauce, so ensure you use the natural juice variety rather than pineapple in syrup.

Quick Duck Cassoulet

Based on a traditional French dish, this hearty meat and bean stew usually takes hours to prepare and cook. This super speedy version tastes great and is ready in a flash.

 **preparation time
10 minutes**

 **cooking time
20 minutes**

567 Kcal per portion

SERVES 4

- **Boneless duck breasts**, 2
- **Pork sausages**, 350g (12oz)
- **Butter**, 25g (1oz)
- **Olive oil**, 1 tbsp
- **Red onion**, 1 large, peeled and chopped
- **Flageolet beans**, 410g can, rinsed
- **Cannellini beans**, 410g can, rinsed
- **Chopped tomatoes with garlic**, 2 x 400g cans
- **Fresh thyme**, a few sprigs, or **dried thyme**, 1 tsp
- **Caster sugar**, 2 tsp
- **Salt and freshly ground black pepper**
- **Flat leaf parsley**, chopped, 2 tbsp

1 Remove the skin from the duck and wash and pat dry. Cut into small pieces. Cut the sausages into thick chunks.

2 Heat the butter with the oil in a large saucepan and gently fry the duck, sausages and onion, stirring, for about 10 minutes until well browned all over.

3 Add the beans, tomatoes, thyme and sugar, bring to the boil and then simmer gently for 10 minutes until the vegetables are tender and the meat cooked through.

4 To serve, adjust seasoning and ladle into warmed shallow bowls. Sprinkle with chopped parsley and serve immediately.

COOK'S TIP
Serve the cassoulet with a good red wine and lots of crusty French bread.

VARIATION
If preferred, you can use boneless, skinless chicken thighs or cubed pork instead of the duck.

Roast Leg of Lamb with Greek Salad

The rich flavours of roast lamb work well when contrasted with the freshness of a simple salad dressed with oil and lemon.

preparation time
5 minutes

cooking time
25 minutes

486 Kcal per portion

SERVES 4

- **Lamb leg, from fillet end,** 600g (1lb 5oz)
- **Salt and freshly ground black pepper**
- **Rosemary,** 2 sprigs
- **Aubergine,** 1, thinly sliced
- **Olive oil,** 4 tbsp
- **Cos lettuce,** 1 heart, washed
- **Rocket leaves,** a handful
- **Feta cheese,** 200g packet, cubed
- **Ripe tomatoes,** 2, cut into large chunks
- **Cucumber,** ½, cut into small cubes
- **Lemon,** 1

1 Preheat the oven to 200°C/400°F/Gas 6. Rub a generous amount of salt into the fat of the lamb. Place it in a small roasting dish and lay the rosemary on top.

2 Roast in a hot oven for 25 minutes, until the lamb is cooked but rosy. When done, remove from the oven to rest for 5 minutes, keeping it warm.

3 While the lamb is roasting, toss the sliced aubergine in 2 tbsp of the olive oil, season and spread out on a non-stick baking tray. Roast for about 10 minutes until tender.

4 Place the lettuce, broken into large pieces, on a platter along with the rocket, feta, tomatoes and cucumber. Pour over the remaining olive oil and a squeeze of lemon juice. Season and toss lightly. Top with the cooked aubergine slices.

5 Carve the lamb into thick slices and lay over the salad. Serve immediately with some good crusty bread.

COOK'S TIP
Other Mediterranean vegetables can be used in this recipe. Roast rounds of courgettes or thin slices of red pepper in the same way as the aubergine.

Pork & Mango Kebabs

Sweet and spicy flavours join together in these quick kebabs.

 preparation time
10 minutes

 cooking time
20 minutes

274 Kcal per portion

SERVES 4
- **Lean pork fillet,** 500g (1lb 2oz)
- **Low-fat natural yogurt,** 6 tbsp
- **Creamed coconut,** 25g (1oz)
- **Garlic clove,** 1
- **Spicy mango chutney,** 2 tbsp
- **Ground turmeric,** 1 tsp
- **Salt and freshly ground black pepper**
- **Ripe mango,** 1 large
- **Lime,** 1, cut into wedges

1 Wash and pat dry the pork fillet, then cut into 2cm (¾in) thick pieces.

2 Place the yogurt in a bowl and grate in the coconut. Peel and crush the garlic and mix into the yogurt along with the chutney, turmeric and seasoning. Add the pork and mix well to coat. Set aside.

3 Peel the mango. Slice down either side of the smooth, flat central stone and cut the mango into large pieces. Then thread the mango and the pork on to 8 skewers, reserving any yogurt mixture that remains in the bowl.

4 Preheat the grill to a medium setting. Arrange the skewers on the grill rack and

cook for 8–10 minutes until browned. Turn over, brush with any reserved yogurt coating and cook for a further 8–10 minutes until tender, golden and cooked through.

5 Serve the pork skewers with wedges of lime to squeeze over and a relish of chopped coriander tomato, cucumber and red onion.

COOK'S TIP

Coating meat in yogurt really helps to tenderise it, so the longer you can leave the meat to marinate the better.

Teriyaki Beef & Orange Skewers

Japanese flavours give these quick and easy kebabs a new twist.

preparation time
20 minutes

cooking time
10 minutes

197 Kcal per portion

SERVES 4

- **Lean beef steak**, 450g (1lb)
- **Oranges**, 2
- **Spring onions**, 1 bunch
- **Garlic clove**, 1, peeled and and finely chopped
- **Root ginger**, 2.5cm (1in) piece, peeled and finely chopped
- **Dark soy sauce**, 2 tbsp
- **Dry sherry**, 1 tbsp
- **Clear honey**, 1 tbsp
- **Sesame oil**, 1 tsp

COOK'S TIP

If time permits, allow the meat to marinate in the soy sauce mixture, covered and chilled, for 2 hours. Replace the beef with chicken if preferred.

Sticky rice is available from any supermarket; follow the manufacturer's instructions for cooking. Jasmine or basmati rice would also work well as they have a delicate 'oriental' fragrance and flavour.

1 Soak 8 bamboo skewers in warm water until required. Meanwhile, trim any visible fat from the beef and cut the meat into small chunks. Place in a shallow dish.

2 Slice off the tops and bottoms from the oranges, then remove the skin and pith. Over the dish containing the beef, slice along the side of the membranes dividing the orange segments, letting the juice and segments fall into the bowl.

3 Trim the spring onions and cut into batons about 5cm (2in) long. Mix into the beef along with the remaining ingredients.

4 Thread the beef onto each skewer interspersed with the orange and spring onion pieces. Reserve the juices. Cover the ends of the skewers with foil to keep the sticks from burning.

5 Preheat the grill to a medium setting. Arrange the skewers on the grill rack and cook for 3–4 minutes on each side, brushing with reserved juices to prevent drying out.

6 Strain the remaining juices into a small saucepan, bring to the boil and simmer for 1–2 minutes until slightly syrupy. Serve the kebabs drizzled with a little syrup, rice and some finely shredded vegetables with bean sprouts.

Steak & Mushrooms with Green Peppercorn Butter

The rich flavour of the steak has added kick from the spicy green peppercorn butter.

 preparation time
15 minutes

 cooking time
15 minutes

375 Kcal per portion

SERVES 4

- **Butter,** 75g (3oz), softened
- **Shallots,** 6
- **Pickled green peppercorns,** 1 tbsp, drained
- **Lean beef steaks, such as sirloin or rump,** 4
- **Salt and freshly ground black pepper**
- **Large flat mushrooms,** 4
- **Olive oil,** 1 tbsp
- **Flat leaf parsley,** chopped, 2 tbsp, to garnish

1 Place 50g (2oz) of the butter in a small bowl. Peel the shallots and finely chop one of them. Mix it into the butter. Lightly crush the peppercorns and mix into the butter. Cover and place in the fridge until required.

2 Meanwhile, slice the remaining shallots. Wash and pat the steaks dry and season on both sides. Peel the mushrooms, if necessary, and then slice thickly.

3 Melt the remaining butter with the oil in a large frying pan and gently cook the shallots for 3–4 minutes until softened.

4 Add the steaks and cook for 5–6 minutes on each side (rare), 7–8 minutes on each side (medium) or 9–10 minutes on each side (well done). Remove the steaks and shallots, reserving the pan juices, and keep warm.

5 Add the mushrooms to the pan, and stir fry for about 3 minutes until just cooked through. Drain.

6 Place the steaks and shallots on warmed serving plates and top with the mushrooms. Sprinkle with chopped parsley and place a knob of the peppercorn butter on top of each. Serve with new potatoes and steamed mange tout.

COOK'S TIP

Look out for green peppercorns pickled in brine in the herb and spice racks of your local grocer, delicatessen or supermarket.

If you don't have a pestle and mortar for crushing spices, place the spice in a small, sturdy bowl and crush with the end of a rolling pin.

Mini Beef Wellingtons

Traditionally made using a whole fillet of beef wrapped in pastry, this classic dish is associated with The Duke of Wellington, as it was said to resemble a highly polished riding boot! These mini-versions make impressive dinner-party fare.

 preparation time
10 minutes

 cooking time
20 minutes

485 Kcal per portion

SERVES 4

- **Lean fillet beef**, 350g (12oz) piece
- **Salt and freshly ground black pepper**
- **Puff pastry**, 250g (9oz), thawed if frozen
- **Coarse pâté**, 110g (4oz)
- **Mushroom pâté**, 50g (2oz)
- **Egg yolk**, 1
- **Milk**, 1 tbsp

1 Preheat the oven to 220°C/425°F/Gas 7. Wash and pat dry the beef and slice into 4 equal steaks. Season on both sides.

2 Roll out the pastry on a lightly floured surface into a 30cm (12in) square. Divide into 4 small squares, and place a portion of coarse pâté in the centre of each.

3 For each parcel, place a piece of beef on top of the pâté, pushing it down, and then top each with a little more mushroom pâté.

4 Mix the egg yolk with the milk and brush the edges of the pastry with the mixture. Fold up the sides like an envelope, pressing on the top to seal.

5 Transfer the parcels, seam-sides down, to a baking sheet lined with baking parchment. Score the tops and brush with the egg and milk mixture. Bake in the oven for 20 minutes until golden. Drain any leaked juices and serve with horseradish sauce, English mustard and some steamed baby carrots, courgette strips and sliced runner beans.

COOK'S TIP

To save time, use ready-rolled puff pastry sheets, which are separated by sheets of non-stick paper. You don't have to use the whole packet at one time, thereby saving money too.

Desserts & Treats

From fresh fruit prepared simply so that its flavour is
honoured and retained to professional-looking sweets that
taste as good as they look, there is something for everyone
in this chapter. For a refreshing end to your meal, you can't
beat Blueberry and Melon Salad (p166), while to impress
guests or pamper yourself try Flambeed Cherries (p170) or
Baked Alaska (p179). Best of all, none of these scrumptious
recipes demands too much preparation or cooking time.

Raspberry Creams

This is the perfect combination of sweet and tart – fresh raspberries between layers of light and fluffy cream.

 preparation time 25 minutes

347 Kcal per portion

SERVES 4

- **Raspberries**, 300g (11oz)
- **Kirsch or Grand Marnier**, 2 tbsp
- **Caster sugar**, 25g (1oz)
- **Double cream**, 242ml pot
- **Egg white**, 1 large
- **Fresh mint leaves**, for decoration

1 Reserving 4 of the raspberries for decoration, place half of the rest in a bowl. Add the Kirsch or Grand Marnier, mix together gently and set aside. Pass the remaining raspberries through a sieve to make a purée. Add the sugar and stir until dissolved.

2 Whisk the double cream until it will just hold a light trail (take care not to over-whisk as it will thicken further when adding the purée). Add the raspberry purée to the cream and fold together very gently.

3 In a separate bowl, whisk the egg white until it will hold a soft, floppy peak and then fold the egg white carefully into the raspberry cream.

4 Spoon half of the raspberry cream into 4 serving glasses, spoon the liqueur-soaked raspberries on top, including juices, then cover with the remaining cream.

5 Cover the glasses with cling film and chill. Just before serving, decorate with mint leaves and reserved raspberries.

COOK'S TIPS

Pregnant women and young children should not eat raw egg.

If the raspberries are very tart, add a little more sugar to the purée, as well as adding some to the liqueur.

Raspberry Crowdie

The toasted oatmeal gives this traditional Scottish dessert a delicate nutty flavour. Crowdie also uses two other famous Scottish products – raspberries and whisky.

preparation time
15 minutes

cooking time
5 minutes

532 Kcal per portion

SERVES 4

- **Medium oatmeal**, 50g (2oz)
- **Double cream**, 300ml (½ pint)
- **Single cream**, 150ml (¼ pint)
- **Soft light brown sugar**, 2 tbsp
- **Whisky**, 3 tbsp
- **Fresh raspberries**, 250g (9oz), plus a few extra for decoration

COOK'S TIP

Although you can chill the crowdie for only 30 minutes, chilling for at least 2 hours allows the oatmeal to soften. Do not chill overnight as the mixture will become too stiff.

VARIATIONS

This Scottish dish is traditionally made with whisky, but you can also use brandy, Grand Marnier or vanilla extract. If using vanilla extract, use 2 tsp rather than the 3 tbsp of whisky in the recipe.

1 Place the oatmeal in a clean, dry frying pan and cook it for about 5 minutes until it has very lightly toasted, shaking and stirring with a fork to prevent the oatmeal from burning. Pour onto a plate and allow to cool.

2 Pour the creams into a bowl, add the sugar and whisky and whisk until the cream just holds a light trail.

3 Add the cold oatmeal and raspberries to the sweetened cream and gently fold together. Spoon into glass dessert dishes or wine glasses, cover with cling film and chill. Serve decorated with raspberries.

Blueberry & Melon Salad

Malmsey Madeira adds a splash of richness to this simple, yet elegant fruit salad.

 preparation time
10 minutes

173 Kcal per portion

SERVES 4

- **Melon(s),** 1 large or 2 small
- **Blueberries,** 250g (9oz)
- **Malmsey Madeira,** 6 tbsp
- **Caster sugar,** 4 tbsp
- **Mint leaves,** to decorate
- **Icing sugar,** for decoration

1 Cut the melon(s) in half and scoop out the seeds, then remove the flesh with a melon baller and put it into a bowl. If using small melons, reserve the halves for serving.

2 Add the blueberries, Madeira and caster sugar to the melon and mix together gently. Cover with all-purpose cling film and leave to stand until ready to serve.

3 Just before serving, spoon the fruit salad into large brandy or wine glasses, which will make it easy for you to drink the delicious juice when you have eaten the salad.

4 Decorate with mint leaves, sift icing sugar over the top and serve immediately.

PLANNING AHEAD

If preparing this salad well ahead of serving time, keep refrigerated – undecorated – until 30 minutes before serving.

VARIATIONS

This salad can be made with Charentaise, Gallia or Ogen melons.

If blueberries are unavailable, make the salad with fresh raspberries instead.

If you haven't got a melon baller, cut the melon into quarters and remove the flesh with a knife. Then cut it into cubes, a little larger than 1cm (½in) across.

Amaretti Cream with Pineapple

Pretty to look at and sinfully rich, this dessert uses Amaretti,
the Italian hazelnut-based macaroon.

 preparation time
15 minutes

480 Kcal per portion

SERVES 4
- **Pineapple**, 1 large
- **Caster sugar**, 1 tbsp
- **Kirsch**, 2 tbsp
- **Double cream**, 250ml (8fl oz)
- **Amaretti**, 50g (2oz), plus 4 halves for decoration
- **Mint leaves**, for decoration

COOK'S TIP
Use the remaining pineapple for making sorbet or to include in a fruit salad.

VARIATIONS
This pretty dessert can also be made with crushed gingernut biscuits.

Use 2 tbsp of Amaretto liqueur, Grand Marnier or brandy instead of kirsch.

1 Cut four 10cm (½in) thick slices from the widest part of the pineapple. The rest will not be needed, but can be used for other purposes.

2 With a 10cm (4in) plain round cutter or sharp knife, cut out a round of pineapple from each slice. Then, with a small round cutter or the same knife, cut out the woody centre cores from the pinapple rings.

3 Place the pineapple rings on 4 serving plates, then cut each one into 8 pieces. Gently open out the segments to form a larger ring, with a centre hole of about 6cm (2½in) diameter, taking care to keep the segments in a neat circle. Sprinkle the sugar over the pineapple, then spoon over the kirsch.

4 Whisk the cream until it holds a soft, floppy peak. Crush the amaretti (in a bowl with the end of a rolling pin) and gently fold into the cream.

5 To serve, spoon the amaretti cream into the centre of the pineapple circles, place amaretti halves on top and decorate with mint leaves.

Speedy Tiramisu

Making tiramisu usually takes hours, but with this speedy version you don't need to wait long to enjoy a delicious 'pick-me-up'.

 **preparation time
20 minutes**

445 Kcal per portion

SERVES 4

- **Strong black coffee,** 4 tbsp
- **Caster sugar,** 1 tsp
- **Brandy,** 2–3 tbsp
- **Italian sponge lady fingers,** 6
- **Mascarpone cheese,** 250g pot
- **Egg,** 1 large
- **Rum,** 2 tbsp
- **Natural vanilla extract,** 1 tsp
- **Icing sugar,** 2 tbsp
- **Chocolate flake bar,** 1, for decoration

COOK'S TIPS

Pregnant women and young children should not eat raw egg.

If you cannot find Italian lady fingers, use 8 regular sponge fingers instead.

1 Put the coffee into a small bowl, add the caster sugar and brandy and stir until the sugar is dissolved.

2 Break the lady fingers in half and place 3 pieces in each of four 375ml (12fl oz) wine glasses. Dividing equally, spoon the coffee mixture over the sponge fingers and set aside to soak while preparing the cream.

3 Place the mascarpone cheese in a bowl. Separate the egg yolk from the white and add the yolk to the mascapone along with the rum, vanilla and icing sugar, then carefully blend together with a wire whisk.

4 In a separate bowl, whisk the egg white until it will hold a soft, floppy peak then carefully fold it into the mascarpone mixture and spoon on top of the sponge fingers.

5 Without unwrapping the chocolate bar, gently crush the flake with your fingers, then open one end and sprinkle the chocolate over the rum cream. Cover the glasses with all-purpose cling film and chill until ready to serve.

Flambéed Cherries

These warm, brandy-flamed cherries are the perfect match for a rich vanilla ice cream.

 preparation time
15 minutes

 cooking time
10 minutes

150 Kcal per portion

SERVES 4

- **Dark red or black cherries**, 450g (1lb)
- **Lemon**, 1 large
- **Caster sugar**, 25g (1oz)
- **Unsalted buttter**, 25g (1oz)
- **Brandy**, 3 tbsp

1 Remove the stones from the fresh cherries with a cherry stoner. Wash the lemon and remove the zest with a zester. Squeeze and strain the juice.

2 Place the caster sugar, butter, lemon zest and juice in a large non-stick frying pan and heat gently until the butter is melted and the sugar dissolved, stirring occasionally.

3 Bring the butter mixture to the boil and allow to bubble gently for about 2 minutes until the mixture begins to thicken and look syrupy, taking care not to let it burn.

4 Add the cherries to the pan and cook gently for another 2 minutes until piping hot and slightly softened. Let the mixture continue to bubble until the liquid is reduced by half.

5 Transfer to a warmed serving dish and pour the brandy over the cherries and ignite with a match. When the flames subside, serve with ice cream or vanilla-flavoured whipped cream.

Apricot & Prune Galettes

These little round fruit tarts look like they've come straight from the bakery.

**preparation time
10 minutes**

**cooking time
15 minutes**

774 Kcal per portion

SERVES 4

- **Apricots,** dried ready-to-eat, 250g (9oz)
- **Prunes,** dried ready-to-eat, 175g (6oz)
- **Brandy,** 3 tbsp
- **Lemon,** 2 tbsp juice
- **Unsalted butter,** 50g (2oz)
- **Fresh puff pastry,** 500g packet
- **Apricot jam,** 3 tbsp
- **Crème fraîche or natural bio yogurt,** 150g (5oz), for serving

1 Preheat the oven to 220°C/425°F/Gas 7. Put the apricots and prunes into a small bowl, add the brandy and lemon juice, mix together gently and set aside. Melt the butter.

2 On a lightly floured surface, roll out the pastry into a 33cm (13in) square. Using a 15cm (6in) saucer as a guide, cut out 4 rounds from the pastry and place on 1 large or 2 small baking sheets. Fold and layer the pastry trimmings, wrap and refrigerate for another use.

3 Brush the pastry rounds with a little of the butter. Drain the juice from the fruit into a small saucepan, then arrange the prunes and apricots on the buttered pastry, dividing equally between the rounds.

4 Brush the remaining butter over the fruit then bake the galettes in the oven for about 15 minutes, until the pastry is well risen, crisp and golden and the fruit is lightly tinged.

5 Meanwhile, add the apricot jam to the strained juice in the small saucepan and stir together over a gentle heat until melted and smooth. Keep hot.

6 When cooked, remove the galettes from the oven and immediately brush them with the apricot glaze. Serve warm, accompanied with crème fraîche or yogurt.

COOK'S TIPS

Puff pasty has many quick uses such as making sausage rolls or jam puffs.

If the pastry was not previously frozen, the trimmings can be frozen and used at a later date.

Apple Fritters

Crisp batter and crunchy cinnamon sugar contrast well with the meltingly soft apple.

 preparation time
10 minutes

 **cooking time**
10 minutes

458 Kcal per portion

SERVES 4

- **Caster sugar**, 50g (2oz)
- **Ground spice, cinnamon or mixed spice,** ½–1 level tsp
- **Plain flour**, 110g (4oz) plus a little extra
- **Salt**
- **Eggs**, 2 large
- **Full cream milk**, 225ml (8fl oz)
- **Corn oil**, 1 litre (1¾ pints)
- **Dessert apples**, 4 large
- **Whipped cream, fromage frais or ice cream,** for serving

1 Mix together the caster sugar and spice in a small bowl. Sift the flour and a good pinch of salt into a larger mixing bowl and make a well in the centre.

2 Separate the egg whites from the yolks and put them into a clean bowl. Place the yolks in the centre of the flour.

3 With a hand-held electric mixer or balloon whisk, gradually whisk the egg yolks into the flour, slowly adding the milk as the mixture thickens. When all the milk has been added and the batter is smooth, set aside.

4 Pour the corn oil into a deep fat frying pan or large saucepan and put on to heat. Meanwhile, put 2–3 tbsp of plain flour on a large plate.

5 Core and peel the apples, then cut each one into 4 thick slices widthways, to make

apple rings. Whisk the egg whites until stiff, but not dry, then fold gently into the batter.

6 To test if the oil is hot enough, drop a small cube of bread into the pan – it should brown evenly within 4–5 seconds. When the oil is hot, lightly coat the apple rings, a few at a time, in the flour (shaking off excess) and then dip in the batter.

7 Using a long skewer, lift the apple rings from the batter and carefully lower them into the hot oil. Cook each batch for 2–3 minutes until they are golden brown, turning the rings over with a slotted spoon when the underside is browned.

8 Drain the fritters well on kitchen paper and keep warm until all the apple rings are cooked. Serve heavily sprinkled with the sugar and spice and accompanied with whipped cream, fromage frais or ice cream.

Baked Plums

As the demerara sugar dissolves into the plum juice, it forms a really delicious syrup.

preparation time
5 minutes

cooking time
20 minutes

642 Kcal per portion

SERVES 4

- **Plums,** 1kg (2lb 4oz)
- **Butter,** 50g (2oz)
- **Demerara sugar,** 110g (4oz)
- **Double cream,** 300ml (½ pint)
- **Caster sugar,** 1 tbsp
- **Kirsch,** 1 tbsp (optional)
- **Elderflower cordial,** 1 tbsp (optional)

COOK'S TIP

When in season, plums such as Marjorie, Seedling, Victoria and Czar are perfect for this delicious dessert – take care not to over-cook the plums, they should soften but still retain their shape, even though some may just start to split.

VARIATION

Instead of Kirsch and elderflower cordial, you might want to add 1 tsp of vanilla extract to flavour the cream.

1 Preheat the oven to 230°C/450°F/Gas 8. Wash and dry the plums and remove their stalks. Melt the butter in a small saucepan and spread out the plums in a single layer on a shallow baking dish.

2 Pour the butter over the plums and turn them over until evenly coated. Sprinkle the demerara sugar evenly over the top of the plums and bake in the oven for 15–20 minutes until the plums are softened and some just start to split – take care not to over-cook them.

3 Meanwhile, whip the cream with the caster sugar and the Kirsch and elderflower cordial, if using. Serve the plums hot accompanied with the whipped cream.

Greek Pastries

The crisp pastry exterior of these flaky triangles conceals a soft, creamy, lemon-scented heart. Luckily, they are easy to make once you've got the hang of folding the triangles.

 preparation time
15 minutes

 cooking time
15 minutes

281 Kcal per pastry

MAKES 8

- **Unsalted butter,** 75g (3oz)
- **Cream cheese,** 150g (5oz)
- **Lemon,** 1 small
- **Caster sugar,** 1 tbsp
- **Egg yolk,** 1
- **Ground cinnamon,** ½ tsp
- **Filo pastry,** 8 sheets, each approximately 18 x 30cm (7 x 12in)
- **Clear honey,** 2 tbsp
- **Greek-style natural yogurt,** for serving

1 Preheat the oven to 200°C/400°F/Gas 6. Grease 1 large or 2 small baking sheets with butter. Melt the 75g (3oz) of butter in a small saucepan and set aside.

2 Place the cream cheese in a small bowl and finely grate the zest from the lemon (or remove with a zester) over the cheese. Then add the sugar, egg yolk and cinnamon and blend well together.

3 Place a sheet of filo on the work surface, with the short ends at the top and bottom. Brush the pastry with some of the melted butter, then cut in half lengthways. Place one half of the sheet on top of the other, to make a long, narrow, double strip.

4 Lightly mark a line in the filo about 7.5cm (3in) down from the top of the strip to mark out a square. Then mark the square diagonally from top left to bottom right, to show two triangles.

5 Take a rounded tsp of the cheese mixture and place it in the centre of the left-hand triangle. Carefully lift up the top right-hand corner of the pastry (both layers together),

bringing it down across the cream cheese to enclose the filling and form a triangle.

6 Take the top left-hand point of the triangle and carefully fold the triangle down to form a straight edge again. Continue to fold the triangle down and from side-to-side to the bottom of the pastry strip to make a neat triangle-shaped package.

7 Place on a baking sheet and brush with butter. Repeat with the remaining filo sheets. Bake the pastries for about 15 minutes until golden brown and crisp. Cool on a wire rack.

8 While the pastries are cooking, squeeze the juice from half of the lemon, put into a small saucepan with the honey and heat gently.

9 Serve the pastries warm as a dessert or tea-time treat, sifted with icing sugar and accompanied with the warmed honey syrup and some Greek-style natural yogurt.

COOK'S TIP
Fresh filo pastry can be found in the chiller cabinets of most supermarkets – it can also be found in freezer cabinets.

Chocolate Sponge Puddings

Rich and chocolatey, these individual puddings cook in just a few minutes in a microwave oven.

 preparation time
10 minutes

 cooking time
10 minutes

652 Kcal per portion

SERVES 4

- **Unsalted butter**, 110g (4oz)
- **Caster sugar**, 110g (4oz)
- **Self-raising flour**, 110g (4oz)
- **Baking powder**, ¼ tsp
- **Cocoa**, 2 tbsp
- **Egg**, 1 large
- **Vanilla extract**, 1 tsp
- **Water**, 2 tbsp

FOR THE SAUCE
- **Dark chocolate**, 110g (4oz)
- **Unsalted butter**, 25g (1oz)
- **Water**, 3 tbsp

COOK'S TIP
If you don't have 4 small pudding basins, large teacups would work just as well.

VARIATION
In addition to the chocolate sauce – or instead of – serve the puddings with whipped cream or ice cream.

1 Thoroughly grease 4 small pudding basins, each with a capacity of 300ml (½ pint), with butter.

2 Place the butter and caster sugar in a mixing bowl, sift the flour, baking powder and cocoa into the bowl, then add the egg, vanilla and water. With an electric hand-held mixer, whisk together the ingredients until smooth.

3 Divide the mixture evenly between the basins, loosely cover with all-purpose cling film and microwave on High for 4–5 minutes until well risen and springy to the touch (cooking time may vary according to the output/category of your oven). Remove from the microwave and leave to stand.

4 While the puddings are cooking, break the chocolate into small pieces and put into a small bowl with the butter and water. Then, while the puddings are standing, microwave the sauce for 1 minute on High. Stir until smooth.

5 Run a palette knife around each pudding to loosen, trim the tops level if necessary and turn the puddings out onto individual plates and coat with the chocolate sauce.

Marmalade Puddings

A steamed pudding is one of the all-time classic desserts; a microwave cooks it in quick time.

 preparation time
10 minutes

 cooking time
10 minutes

572 Kcal per portion

SERVES 4

- **Traditional marmalade,** 200g (7oz)
- **Unsalted butter,** 110g (4oz)
- **Soft light brown sugar,** 110g (4oz)
- **Orange,** 1
- **Self-raising flour,** 110g (4oz)
- **Baking powder,** ¼ tsp
- **Egg,** 1 large

COOK'S TIP
If you don't have 4 small pudding basins, large teacups would work just as well.

VARIATION
You can also serve these tangy puddings with custard, or use lemon curd instead of marmalade if preferred.

1 Thoroughly grease 4 small pudding basins, each with a capacity of 300ml (½ pint), with butter and spoon the marmalade into the bottom, dividing it equally.

2 Place the butter and sugar into a mixing bowl. Remove the zest from the orange with a zester and add it to the bowl. Squeeze and strain the juice from the orange.

3 Sift the flour and baking powder into the bowl, add the egg and 2 tbsp of the orange juice. With an electric hand-held electric mixer, whisk together the ingredients until smooth.

4 Divide the mixture evenly between the basins on top of the marmalade. Loosely cover with all-purpose cling film and microwave on High for 4–5 minutes until well risen and springy to the touch (cooking time may vary according to the output/ category of your oven). Remove from the microwave and leave to stand for 1 minute.

5 Run a palette knife around each pudding to loosen, trim the tops level if necessary and turn the puddings out onto individual plates.

Summer Fruit Baked Alaska

*The magic of a baked Alaska, straight from the oven but still
frozen inside, never fails to impress. This one takes just minutes to
assemble and is perfect for summer entertaining.*

 **preparation time
20 minutes**

 **cooking time
2 minutes**

825 Kcal per portion

SERVES 6

- **Strawberries,** 300g (11oz)
- **Raspberries,** 175g (6oz)
- **Blueberries,** 100g (3½oz)
- **Caster sugar,** 400g (14oz)
- **Bought sponge flan case,**
  25cm (10in) diameter
- **Maple syrup,** 6 tbsp
- **Egg whites,** 6 large
- **Vanilla ice cream,** 1 litre
  block

1 Preheat the oven to 230°C/450°F/Gas 8. Hull and slice the
strawberries and put into a large bowl with the raspberries
and blueberries and 50g (2oz) of the sugar. Mix gently and set
aside for 10 minutes.

2 Place the flan case on a large ovenproof plate and drizzle
over the maple syrup.

3 Whisk the egg whites in a large bowl or food mixer until stiff,
then gradually whisk in the remaining caster sugar (a tbsp at
a time, whisking well between each addition) to make a stiff
shiny meringue.

4 Spoon the fruits into the flan case, spread evenly and place
the ice cream on top. Completely cover the ice cream with
the meringue and mark it into swirls – making sure that there are
no gaps left.

5 Flash bake the Alaska in the centre of the oven for 1–2
minutes until lightly browned. Remove from the oven and
serve immediately.

COOK'S TIPS

To ensure a good consistency of the meringue mixture, use a
greasefree ceramic or metal bowl – it is best to avoid plastic.

Be sure to keep the ice cream in the freezer until the meringue
is made.

You don't use the egg yolks in this recipe so pour a little water
over them to keep them fresh and refrigerate until you are
ready to make some pastry, assuming this will be within 3 days.

Brandy Snap Baskets with Chocolate & Coffee Cream

Chocolate and coffee are strongly contrasting flavours and yet they complement each other superbly well.

 preparation time
15 minutes

 cooking time
5 minutes

536 Kcal per portion

SERVES 4
- **Dark chocolate**, 75g (3oz)
- **Water**, 2 tbsp
- **Brandy**, 1 tbsp
- **Egg yolk**, 1 large
- **Double cream**, 300ml (½ pint)
- **Strong black coffee**, 1 tbsp
- **Caster sugar**, 2 tsp
- **Vanilla extract**, ½ tsp
- **Brandy snap baskets**, 4
- **A few pink rose petals**, for decoration
- **Icing sugar**, 2 tsp, for decoration

1 Break the chocolate into small pieces and put into a small bowl with the water and brandy. Place the bowl over a pan of gently simmering water and stir until all the chocolate has completely melted.

2 Stir the egg yolk into the melted chocolate until smooth, then set aside to cool, but do not allow to set.

3 Divide the double cream equally between two mixing bowls. Add the coffee, caster sugar and vanilla to one of the bowls and whisk until the cream holds slightly stiff peaks.

4 Whisk the remaining cream until it holds soft peaks, then fold in the cooled chocolate. If necessary, after adding the chocolate, whisk the cream again until it holds a peak.

5 Spoon the creams alternately into the brandy snap baskets placed on individual serving plates. Cover with small up-turned bowls and chill until ready to serve.

6 Just before serving, sprinkle the contents of each basket with rose petals and sift lightly with icing sugar.

COOK'S TIPS

Brandy snap baskets can be bought, ready made, from most good supermarkets.

A very attractive effect can be obtained by putting both creams together in a large piping bag fitted with a large star nozzle (coffee on one side of the bag, chocolate on the other) then piping the mixture in large swirls into the baskets to create a two-tone effect.

Peanut Brittle

Children and adults alike love the caramel taste of peanut brittle.

 preparation time
5 minutes

 cooking time
15 minutes

118 Kcal per 25g (1oz)

MAKES 425g (15oz)

- **Caster sugar,** 175g (6oz)
- **Golden syrup,** 75g (3oz)
- **Water,** 125ml (4fl oz)
- **Natural shelled peanuts,** 175g (6oz)
- **Unsalted butter,** 15g (½oz)

1 Using a flavourless oil, such as sunflower oil, lightly oil a baking tray, preferably non-stick.

2 Put the sugar and golden syrup into heavy-based saucepan and add the cold water. Fill a jug or small bowl with boiling water.

3 Place the saucepan over a moderate heat and stir continuously until every granule of sugar is dissolved, brushing the sides of the pan down with the hot water from time-to-time. If the sugar is not properly dissolved the mixture will crystallise.

4 When the sugar is completely dissolved, add the peanuts to the sugar syrup and bring to the boil. Then boil, without stirring, until the mixture turns to a rich, golden, caramel colour, taking care not to let it burn. The colour test is important because if it is not sufficiently dark, the brittle will not set.

5 Immediately the mixture turns to a rich caramel colour, remove the pan from the heat and swirl in the butter by gently moving the pan by its handle. Do not stir the mixture. Then quickly pour onto the prepared baking tray and leave to cool and set hard.

6 When cold, break the brittle into small pieces with a toffee hammer or heavy kitchen weight. Store in an airtight tin in single layers between sheets of waxed or non-stick baking paper.

COOK'S TIPS

Ensure you buy unsalted peanuts!

A heavy-based saucepan is preferable for making this brittle and try to use a stainless steel one so you can see the colour of the syrup clearly as it changes from clear to caramel.

Fruit & Muesli Crumble

This versatile crumble can be made with virtually any fruit you like such as fresh or frozen gooseberries, Black Forest fruits or fresh apples or plums.

**preparation time
5 minutes**

**cooking time
25 minutes**

438 Kcal per portion

SERVES 4

- **Frozen Black Forest fruits,** 500g pack
- **Caster sugar,** 50g (2oz)
- **Butter,** 75g (3oz)
- **Golden syrup,** 50g (2oz)
- **Natural muesli,** 175g (6oz)
- **Icing sugar,** 1 tbsp, for decoration

1 Preheat the oven to 200°C/400°C/Gas 6. Place the frozen fruits in a shallow, round baking dish (22–23cm/8½–9 in diameter), sprinkle with the caster sugar and mix together gently. Place the fruit in the centre of the oven to start cooking while you prepare the topping.

2 Put the butter and golden sryup into a large saucepan and stir together until melted, then stir in the muesli and remove from heat.

3 When the fruit has been cooking for approximately 10 minutes and is starting to soften, remove from oven and spoon the muesli mixture evenly over the top.

4 Return the dish to the oven and continue cooking the crumble for about 15 minutes until the muesli is golden brown and the fruit is bubbling hot.

5 Sift icing sugar over the crumble and serve, accompanied with ice cream or whipped cream.

Basic Recipes

You can buy some delicious ready-made sauces and ingredients, but what tastes better than something you've made yourself? As well as the satisfaction of having created your own meals, you also know exactly what you have put into it.

DRESSINGS

French dressing

Everyone has their own way for making French dressing. Here is a basic recipe to which you can add your own ingredients, as described in the variations given beneath this recipe.

- **Olive oil,** 4 tbsp
- **White wine vinegar,** 2 tbsp
- **Dry mustard,** ½ tsp
- **Salt and freshly ground black pepper**

1 Put all the ingredients into a bowl, adding the seasoning to taste. Whisk until thoroughly blended. Transfer to a bottle or jug and shake or stir before each use.

VARIATIONS

- In place of the wine vinegar, use half wine vinegar, half lemon juice – or all lemon juice if you prefer.
- Add some dried chilli flakes for something a bit spicier.
- Add some of your favourite herbs such as rosemary or basil.
- Add some finely chopped garlic.

Mayonnaise

A home-made mayonnaise is a real treat but take your time when adding the oil as it will curdle all too easily. Ensure all your ingredients are at room temperature too as this will also help prevent curdling.

- **Egg yolks,** 2
- **Dry mustard,** ½ tsp
- **Salt,** ½ tsp
- **Freshly ground black pepper**
- **Worcestershire sauce,** ¼ tsp (optional)
- **Olive oil,** 300ml (½ pint)
- **Vinegar or lemon juice,** 2 tbsp
- **Hot water,** 1 tbsp

1 Place the egg yolks, mustard, salt, pepper and Worcestershire sauce (if using) in a bowl. Beat until smooth.
2 Beating more quickly, add 150ml (¼ pint) of the oil very slowly, a drop at a time, and continue beating until the mayonnaise is very thick.
3 Stir in 1 tbsp of the vinegar or lemon juice. Then beat in the remaining oil gradually, about 2 tsp at a time.
4 When all the oil has been added, stir in the remaining vinegar or lemon juice and the hot water (water helps prevent separation). Add seasoning.
5 Transfer to a covered container and store in the refrigerator where it will keep for up to 2 weeks.

VARIATIONS

Make each of these variations by adding the necessary ingredients to the recipe above after you have stirred in the hot water. Or buy a jar of mayonnaise and add these to its contents.

- Thousand island mayonnaise: 4 tsp tomato ketchup, 4 tbsp double cream and ½ tsp chilli sauce.
- Garlic mayonnaise (aioli): 1 garlic clove, crushed.

Soured cream dressing

Make this creamy dressing to accompany a salad or as a dip for fresh carrots, cucumber and celery sticks.

- **Soured cream,** 150ml (5 fl oz)
- **Milk,** 1 tbsp
- **Lemon juice,** 1 tbsp
- **Salt and freshly ground black pepper**

1 Beat the soured cream together with the milk and lemon juice. Season to taste.
2 For a thinner dressing, add a little extra milk.
3 Leave to stand for 15 minutes before using to allow the flavour to develop.

VARIATIONS

Before the dressing stands, add any one of the following ingredients.

- Parsley, chopped, 3 tbsp
- Wholegrain mustard, 1 tsp
- Creamed horseradish sauce, 1 tbsp
- Tomato ketchup, 2 tbsp
- Paprika, 2 tsp blended with 2 tsp fresh milk
- Blue Stilton cheese: 50g (2oz) mashed in 1 tbsp fresh milk

PASTRY

Shortcrust pastry

When a recipe calls for a certain weight of pastry and it is home-made pastry, the weight refers to the amount of flour used and not to the total amount of pastry.

For example, if a recipe says you need 110g (4oz) shortcrust pastry, it means you start off with 110g (4oz) flour and then add the other ingredients.

But when a recipe asks for a certain weight of bought pastry, this refers to the total weight.

For example, if a recipe says you need 225g (8oz) puff pastry, you should buy just that.

- **Plain flour,** 225g (8oz)
- **Salt,** ¼ tsp
- **Butter,** 110g (4oz)
- **Cold water,** 1–1½ tsp per 25g (1oz) flour

1 Sift the flour and salt into a bowl. Add the butter and cut it into the flour with a knife.
2 Rub in the butter with your fingertips until the mixture looks like fine breadcrumbs.
3 Sprinkle most of the water over the crumbs and mix to a stiff, crumbly-looking paste with a round-ended knife, adding more water if necessary.
4 Draw together the pastry with the fingertips, turn out on to a lightly floured work surface and knead quickly until smooth and crack free.
5 Roll out and use the pastry as required.

Wholemeal shortcrust pastry

This recipe is a wholemeal version of the basic shortcrust recipe.

- **Wholemeal flour,** 110g (4oz)
- **Self-raising wholemeal flour,** 110g (4oz)
- **Pinch of salt**
- **Butter,** 110g (4oz)
- **Water,** 100ml (4fl oz)

1 Put the flours, salt and butter into a bowl. Rub the butter into the flour until the mixture resembles fine breadcrumbs.
2 Add water over the crumbs and mix with a round-ended knife to a soft dough.
3 Draw together the pastry with the fingertips and leave the dough in a bowl and refrigerate for 5 minutes.
4 Roll out and use the pastry as required.

PASTRY HINTS AND TIPS

- Savoury pastry is perfect for flan, pie and quiche bases, or pie coverings.
- If you are making a sweet pie, you might wish to add 1 tbsp caster sugar to the pastry mixture.
- When making pastry, keep everything as cool as possible, including your hands.
- Before rolling out pastry it is best to chill it in the refrigerator for 30 minutes wrapped in all-purpose cling film. This makes the pastry more pliable and elastic and so easier to roll out and cook without shrinking.

SAUCES

White sauce

A classic recipe that is a staple for any cook, to be used on its own or with added ingredients.
- **Butter,** 15g (½oz)
- **Flour,** 15g (½oz)
- **Milk,** 300ml (½ pint)
- **Salt and freshly ground black pepper**

1 Melt the butter in a saucepan. Add the flour and cook over a low heat, stirring, for 2 minutes. Do not allow the mixture (roux) to brown.
2 Gradually blend in the milk. Cook, stirring, until the sauce thickens, boils and is smooth.
3 Simmer gently for 3 minutes and season to taste.

VARIATIONS

- Cheese sauce: Before seasoning, stir in 50g (2oz) grated mature Cheddar cheese or 50g (2oz) crumbled Lancashire cheese, 1 tsp mustard and a pinch of cayenne pepper.
- Lemon sauce: Before seasoning, stir in the grated zest of 1 small lemon and 1 tbsp lemon juice. Reheat gently before using.
- Prawn sauce: Before seasoning, stir in 50g (2oz) pre-cooked, peeled prawns and ½ tsp dry mustard mixed with 1 tsp lemon juice. Reheat gently before using.
- To make an even quicker, one-stage white sauce, follow the recipe above for basic white sauce. Put the butter, flour and milk into a saucepan. Heat, whisking continuously, until the sauce thickens, boils and is smooth. Season to taste.

Béchamel

A béchamel sauce is a richer version of the white sauce given on the previous page. Its flavour is further enhanced by infusing the milk first for about 30 minutes, as explained in the method given below.

- **Milk**, 300ml (½ pint)
- **Onion**, 1 small, peeled and quartered
- **Carrot**, 1 small, peeled and sliced
- **Celery stick**, ½ small, sliced
- **Cloves**, 2
- **Peppercorns**, 6
- **Mace**, ½ tsp
- **Parsley**, chopped, 1 tbsp
- **Butter**, 25g (1oz)
- **Flour**, 25g (1oz)
- **Salt and freshly ground black pepper**
- **Double cream**, 2 tbsp

1 Put the milk into a saucepan. Add the onion, carrot, celery, cloves, peppercorns, mace and parsley and slowly bring just to the boil.
2 Remove from the heat and cover. Leave to stand for 30 minutes then strain and reserve the flavoured milk.
3 Melt the butter in the pan, add the flour and cook over a low heat, stirring, for 2 minutes. Do not allow the mixture (roux) to brown.
4 Gradually blend in the flavoured milk and cook, stirring, until the sauce thickens, boils and is smooth. Simmer gently for 3 minutes. Remove from the heat, season and stir in the cream.

Hollandaise sauce

A perfect Hollandaise sauce takes time and patience.

In this book, a recipe is given on page 17 for a quicker and simpler version. Here is another recipe, which is guaranteed to work each time.

1 Start by following the recipe and method for the Béchamel sauce given to the left.
2 But before seasoning and rather than stirring in cream alone, stir in 1 egg yolk mixed with 2 tbsp double cream and 2 tsp lemon juice.
3 Reheat gently and do not allow to boil.

Tomato sauce

It is also useful to have a batch of tomato sauce in the fridge or freezer. It is perfect to serve with pasta or add to other recipes as flavouring.

- **Butter**, 25g (1oz)
- **Vegetable oil**, 1 tsp
- **Onion**, 1, peeled and chopped
- **Garlic clove**, 1, peeled and crushed
- **Chopped tomatoes**, 400g can
- **Tomato purée**, 1 tbsp
- **Vegetable stock**, 300ml (½ pint)
- **Mace**, ground, ¼ tsp
- **Mixed herbs**, dried, 2 tsp
- **Freshly ground black pepper**

1 Heat the butter and oil in a saucepan. Add the onion and garlic and fry for about 2 minutes until golden.
2 Stir in the tomatoes, tomato purée, stock, mace and herbs and season to taste.
3 Bring to the boil, continuously stirring. Reduce the heat, cover, and simmer gently for 20 minutes.

The perfect gravy

Everyone has their own ideas about how the perfect gravy should taste, but not everyone knows how to make it, so follow the instructions given below and you will soon be creating delicious gravy to accompany your favourite Sunday roast.

- **Fat and sediment from roasting tin**
- **Cornflour**, 1 tbsp
- **Stock or vegetable water**, 300 ml (½ pint)
- **Red wine**, 150 ml (¼ pint)
- **Salt and freshly ground black pepper**
- **Mustard**, 1 tsp

1 Pour off all but 1 tbsp fat from the roasting tin but ensure you keep all the sediment and occasional pieces of meat stuck to the base of the tin.
2 Add the cornflour and mix with the fat and sediment. Stand the tin over a low heat and gradually blend in the stock or vegetable water.
3 Cook, stirring, until the gravy comes to the boil and thickens. Add the red wine (with more stock or vegetable water as necessary), seasoning and mustard. Lower the heat and simmer for 3 minutes.

SWEET SAUCES

Chocolate sauce
Make this recipe to serve with whatever takes your fancy.

- **Cornflour**, 1 tbsp
- **Milk**, 300ml (½ pint)
- **Plain chocolate**, 50g (2oz), grated
- **Vanilla essence**, ½ tsp
- **Butter**, 15g (½oz)
- **Caster sugar**, 1 tbsp

1 In a bowl mix the cornflour to a smooth paste with a little of the milk. Put the remaining milk into a saucepan and add the chocolate. Heat until the chocolate melts. Pour onto the cornflour and mix well.
2 Return to the pan. Cook, stirring, until the sauce comes to the boil and thickens. Add the vanilla, butter and sugar and simmer for 3 minutes.

Rich chocolate sauce
For something more luxurious, use this recipe instead.

- **Plain chocolate**, 175g (6oz)
- **Butter**, 20g (¾oz)
- **Water**, 3 tbsp
- **Golden syrup**, 3 tbsp
- **Vanilla essence**, 1 tsp

1 Break the chocolate into small pieces and place in a saucepan with the butter, water and golden syrup.
2 Heat gently until the chocolate has melted. Remove from the heat, add the vanilla essence and stir to mix. Serve while warm.

FOOD SAFETY AND HYGIENE
- Always wash your hands before handling any food.
- Ensure your work surfaces and chopping boards are clean. It is best to keep a separate chopping board for preparing raw meat.
- Read and follow the use-by dates on the packaging.
- If you are reheating food, make sure you heat it all the way through and until it is piping hot.
- Once thawed, do not refreeze raw food unless you have cooked it first.
- Do not buy cracked eggs.
- Pregnant women or the elderly shouldn't eat recipes that contain raw eggs.
- Change and wash tea towels, towels, dishcloths, aprons and oven gloves often.
- Keep your pets off work surfaces and tables.
- Ensure that your fridge is 5°C or less and the deep freeze is at least −20°C.
- Organise your fridge so that meat is kept separately and on the bottom shelf. Keep dairy produce together and fruit, vegetables and salad ingredients in the salad compartment.
- Store raw foods separately from cooked foods to avoid contamination.
- After shopping, put all food for the refrigerator and freezer into their allotted places as soon as possible.

Cook's Information

Metric and imperial measurements are given in all the recipes. Follow one or the other set and do not mix the two as they are not interchangeable.

Unless otherwise specified, in the recipes in this book always use: medium-sized eggs, fruit and vegetables and fresh herbs.

DRY WEIGHT CONVERSIONS

METRIC	IMPERIAL
15g	½oz
25g	1oz
40g	1½oz
50g	2oz
75g	3oz
100g/110g	4oz
150g	5oz
175g	6oz
200g	7oz
225g	8oz (½lb)
250g	9oz
275g	10oz
300g	11oz
350g	12oz (¾lb)
375g	13oz
400g	14oz
425g	15oz
450g	16oz (1lb)
500g	1lb 2oz
680g	1lb 8oz
900g	2lb
1kg	2lb 4oz
1.125kg	2lb 8oz
1.25kg	2lb 12oz
1.5kg	3lb 5oz
2kg	4lb 8oz
2.25kg	5lb
2.5kg	5lb 8oz
3kg	6lb 8oz

LIQUID CONVERSIONS

METRIC	IMPERIAL	US CUPS
15ml	½fl oz	1 tbsp
30ml	1fl oz	⅛ cup
60ml	2fl oz	¼ cup
90ml	3fl oz	⅜ cup
125ml	4fl oz	½ cup
150ml	5fl oz (¼ pint)	⅔ cup
175ml	6fl oz	¾ cup
250ml	8fl oz	1 cup
300ml	10fl oz (½ pint)	1¼ cups
375ml	12fl oz	1½ cups
450ml	15fl oz	1¾ cups
500ml (½ litre)	16fl oz	2 cups
600ml	20fl oz (1pint)	2½ cups
750ml	1¼ pints	3⅓ cup
900ml	1½ pints	3¾ cups
1 litre	1¾ pints	4 cups (1 qt)
1.25 litres	2 pints	5 cups
1.5 litres	2½ pints	3 US pints
2 litres	3½ pints	2 quarts

TEASPOON AND TABLESPOON MEASURES

Use a set of measuring spoons for teaspoons and tablespoons, and make sure that they are levelled off, unless otherwise stated.

1 tsp = 5ml
2 tsp = 10ml
3 tsp = 1 tbsp = 15ml

OVEN TEMPERATURES

°C	°F	GAS MARK
110	225	¼
120/130	250	½
140	275	1
150	300	2
160/170	325	3
180	350	4
190	375	5
200	400	6
220	425	7
230	450	8
240	475	9

Please note that all oven temperatures vary and so cooking times may differ from those given in the recipes. Do check your manufacturer's handbook, especially if you have a fan-assisted oven.

GUIDE TO ROASTING TIMES FOR MEAT
Set oven temperature to 180°C/350°F/Gas 4.

BEEF	cooking time per 450g/1lb	extra cooking time
Rare	20 min	20 min
Medium	25 min	25 min
Well done	30 min	30 min

LAMB	cooking time per 450g/1lb	extra cooking time
Medium	25 min	25 min
Well done	30 min	30 min

PORK	cooking time per 450g/1lb	extra cooking time
Medium	30 min	30 min
Well done	35 min	35 min

Let the cooked meat rest for 5–15 minutes before carving to allow the juices to be reabsorbed and to make carving easier.

GUIDE TO GRILLING TIMES FOR FISH

type of fish	grilling time
Cod (steak)	5–6 min each side
Dover sole (whole)	4–6 min each side
Dover sole (fillet)	2–3 min each side
Halibut (steak)	5–6 min each side
Herring (whole)	4–5 min each side
Mackerel (whole)	6–7 min each side
Monkfish (steak)	5–6 min each side
Plaice (whole)	4–6 min each side
Plaice (fillet)	2–3 min each side
Salmon (steak)	5–6 min each side
Swordfish (steak)	4–6 min each side
Tuna (steak)	1–2 min each side

Times given for fish weighing approximately 175–225g (6–8oz).

GUIDE TO ROASTING TIMES FOR POULTRY

CHICKEN

oven temperature	cooking time per 450g/1lb	extra cooking time	resting time
200°C/400°F/Gas 6	20 min	30 min	15 min

TURKEY *(stuffed weight)*

oven temperature	cooking time per 450g/1lb	extra cooking time	resting time
small (under 6kg/13lb) 200°C/400°F/Gas 6	12 min	20 min	30 min
large 180°C/350°F/Gas 4	16 min	—	30 min

DUCK

oven temperature	cooking time per 450g/1lb	extra cooking time	resting time
200°C/400°F/Gas 6 for 45 min, then 180°C/350°F/Gas 4	35 min	—	15 min

GUIDE TO STEAMING TIMES FOR VEGETABLES

type of vegetable	steaming time
Asparagus	5–7 min
Beansprouts	3 min
Beetroot (sliced)	5–7 min
Broccoli (florets)	5–7 min
Brussel sprouts	5–7 min
Cabbage (chopped)	4–6 min
Cauliflower (florets)	5–7 min
Carrots (thickly sliced)	5–7 min
Carrots (thinly sliced)	3–5 min
Courgettes (sliced)	3–5 min
Green beans	5–7 min
Kale	3–5 min
Mangetout peas	3–5 min
Spring greens	3–5 min
Parsnips (sliced)	5–7 min
Peas	3–5 min
Potatoes (cubed)	5–7 min
Spinach	3–5 min
Sprouting broccoli	5–7 min

Times given are for steaming from when water has started to boil.

Index